Romans Personal Workbook

By Chad Sychtysz

© 2024 Spiritbuilding Publishers.
All rights reserved. No part of this book may be reproduced in any form without the written permission of the publisher.

Published by
Spiritbuilding Publishers
9700 Ferry Road, Waynesville, Ohio 45068

ROMANS PERSONAL WORKBOOK
By Chad Sychtysz

ISBN: 978-1955285-88-9

Spiritbuilding
PUBLISHERS

spiritbuilding.com

Table of Contents

Introduction to *Romans* 1
Lesson 1: Salutation and Introduction (1:1–17) 3
Section One: The Righteous Are Justified by Faith (1:18—4:25)
Lesson 2: Gentiles Stand Guilty before God (1:18–32) 6
Lesson 3: God Is an Impartial Judge (2:1–16) 11
Lesson 4: Jews Also Stand Guilty before God (2:17–29) 15
Lesson 5: All Have Sinned and Are Guilty before God (3:1–20) 18
Lesson 6: We Are Justified by Grace through Faith (3:21–31) 22
Lesson 7: Historical Examples of Justification by Faith (4:1–25) 25
Section Two: Benefits of Being Justified by Faith (5:1—8:39)
Lesson 8: The Benefit of Peace with God (5:1–21) 29
Lesson 9: The Benefit of Newness of Life (6:1–23) 35
Lesson 10: The Benefit of Freedom from Law's Condemnation (7:1–25) 40
Lesson 11: The Benefit of the Spirit's Guidance (8:1–17) 45
Lesson 12: The Consolation of Hope and Divine Assurance (8:18–39) 50
A Recap of Romans 1—8
Section Three: The Righteousness of God (9:1—11:36)
Lesson 13: God Has Not Failed in His Promises to Israel (9:1–33) 56
Lesson 14: God's Righteousness Shown to Israel (10:1–21) 62
Lesson 15: God's Righteousness Shown to Gentiles (11:1–36) 66
Section Four: The Righteousness of God Produces a Righteous Life (12:1—15:33)
Lesson 16: Righteous Conduct toward Fellow Christians (12:1–21) 71
Lesson 17: Righteous Conduct toward Secular Government (13:1–14) 76
Lesson 18: Righteous Conduct of the Strong and Weak (14:1—15:33) 81
Lesson 19: A Proper Regard for Paul's Ministry (15:14–33) 86
Lesson 20: Paul's Greetings and Final Admonitions (16:1–27) 90
Sources Used for *Romans Personal Workbook* 95
Endnotes 97

Introduction to *Romans*

There is no single book in the New Testament (NT) which provides as much detail and insight into Christian theology as *Romans*. This epistle delves into several critical themes: salvation, grace, mercy, faith, justification by faith, sin, redemption, man's free will, God's sovereign decisions, indwelling of the Holy Spirit, etc. It also provides practical application of these doctrines in the sphere of everyday Christian life (chapters 12—15).

However, as with all doctrinal treatises, *Romans* is admittedly an involved study. The fact that Paul took eight chapters to explain one statement, "the righteous man shall live by faith" (1:17), indicates that this is not going to be a casual read. Yet, this does not mean that Christians should avoid it. In it, Paul explains how (and why) an all-powerful God can and will accept into His fellowship those who are deserving of death. This bears directly upon God's faithfulness to all who are in covenant with Him.

Romans was written ca. AD 57. (Some scholars set the date as early as 56, others as late as 59.) The apostle Paul is unanimously accepted as its author. It is likely that Paul wrote this treatise during his three-month stay in Corinth (in Achaia) during his third missionary journey (Acts 18:23ff), while waiting to return to Jerusalem after a lengthy absence. Having collected money for about a year from among the (predominantly) Gentile churches throughout Macedonia and Achaia, Paul's mission was to provide that money as benevolence toward the famine-stricken Christians in Jerusalem. Afterward, he had every intention of visiting the Christians in Rome (15:22–29). Yet, Paul was arrested in Jerusalem on a false premise and, after spending some two years in jail in Caesarea, was sent to Rome as a prisoner, not as a free man (Acts 21—28).

Theme and Purpose: The theme of *Romans* is undoubtedly "the righteous man shall live by faith" (1:17). Paul not only expounded upon this expression but explained that it is the foundational premise upon which every soul—both Jew and Gentile—is saved. The first eight chapters of *Romans* deal directly with this question in a manner that highlights Paul's intense rabbinical training. The next several chapters (9—11) address how this statement affects the Jews, and subsequently the Gentiles. Both Jews and

Gentiles needed to know exactly where they stood with God and with each other in this new world order called Christianity.

In the final chapters (12—15), Paul provides a practical explanation of how those who live by faith ought to conduct themselves, especially toward their fellow brethren, world governments, the "weak," and all men. Paul ends with a lengthy salutation, as well as necessary warnings and final admonitions to Christians in Rome.

Lesson One:
Salutation and Introduction (1:1–17)

Paul begins his epistle to the Romans with a powerful description of his own apostleship as well as that of Christ (1:1–2). An "apostle" is "one sent forth or away with orders."[1] The term can be used generally (as in Acts 14:14 regarding Barnabas) or specifically (as Paul uses the term here). All of Christ's apostles were ordained ("called") by Christ Himself, being entrusted with His gospel to preach and defend as His personal ambassadors (see Acts 26:16–18).

Though an apostle, Paul regards himself also as a "bond-servant" of Christ. Since Rome was filled with slaves, many of whom were educated even more than their own masters, Paul reminds the Romans that he also is a slave to the Highest Master. Thus, he immediately identifies with the slave population of the Roman Empire by stating, in essence, "I, too, am a slave—to Christ, not to mere men."

Paul then defines the two-fold nature of Christ (1:3–4): according to the flesh, He is "a descendant of David"; according to heaven, He is "the Son of God." To be the King of the Jews, Jesus had to be a legitimate son of David; to be the legitimate Messiah of prophecy, He had to be the only beloved Son of God (Mat. 16:16, John 20:31).

Having established his apostolic authority, Paul's first proclamation is both powerful and positive: he identifies the Roman Christians as "the called of Christ" (1:6), "beloved of God," and "saints" (1:7). Their relationship with God was unquestioned; the rest of the epistle will deal with *how* that relationship came to be and it expects of those who are in it.

Paul's Personal Remarks (1:8–15): Before proceeding to doctrinal matters, Paul first takes a moment to address these Christians on a personal level (1:8–15). He was anxious to see them; it was his full intention to make a brief visit to Rome on his way to Spain (see 15:22–29).[2] It was also his intention to "impart some spiritual gift" to them (1:11)—i.e., to lay his hands upon them for the purpose of giving them miraculous gifts. Thus, he apologized, in a way, for not having already seen them, yet clarified that it was not for lack of desire but of time and opportunity (1:13).

Paul's Thesis: Justification by Faith (1:16–17): In 1:16–17, Paul begins an important theological discussion that will cover the next ten chapters. Despite the low opinion some people had of him (1 Cor. 4:8–13, 2 Cor. 10:10, etc.), Paul was "not ashamed of the gospel" (1:16). "Ashamed" is twofold: first, Paul had no reason to be embarrassed by who he was (a Christian) or what he preached (the gospel). Second, he would not be disappointed or experience regret for having accepted this responsibility. The Greek word for "ashamed" can mean either or both thoughts, and is used both ways in the NT.

The gospel is a message of "salvation"—a state of existence that is entirely beyond human ability to achieve by one's own strength or wisdom. "Power of God" does not refer to the mere *words* of the gospel, as though the Bible has regenerating power of its own. Rather, it is in the "living and enduring word of God" (1 Peter 1:23)—i.e., the divine message of the Holy Spirit, which, when obeyed, calls for divine grace to heal an otherwise helpless human soul. This power is universal in scope: it is available to Jews and non-Jews alike. Yet, it remains particular or conditional in its application: only those who "believe" with obedient faith receive it.

Paul says "to the Jew first" because entrance into God's kingdom was the culmination of promises made to the kingdom of Israel. The fact that many Jews did not accept Jesus as their King—and thus rejected this invitation (see Acts 13:45–47)—did not diminish the power of the kingdom or God's decision to invite them "first." God also invited the "Greek," which can mean a Greek-speaking person, a cultured (Hellenistic) Greek, or simply a non-Jew (i.e., a Gentile). In short, this gospel is available to the entire world, to "whoever believes in Him" (John 3:16).

"For in it [i.e., the gospel] the righteousness of God is revealed" (1:17)—that is, God's fairness, justice, grace, and mercy are all made supremely evident within this message of salvation. Whenever Paul says, "God is faithful" (1 Cor. 1:9), he is also saying, "God is righteous," for it is impossible for Him to be one without the other. Through the terms of His gospel, God can justify those who have faith in Him, and because of this justification, they also can be righteous as He is. This is how sinners have *always* been justified by God: through *faith*, not mere works, good intentions, or any other means.

Questions

1.) Is Paul's apostolic authority still a relevant issue? Why or why not?

2.) What is the connection between "obedience" and "faith" (1:5)? Is one acceptable to God without the other or are they both required at the same time?

3.) Faith, as defined in Scripture, requires some point of reference—a thing or person in which that faith is placed.

   a. Given this, what is wrong with a person who merely says, "I have faith" or "I am faithful"? With no point of reference, what good *is* that faith?

   b. On the other hand, if one claims to have faith in God (whose rank and authority far exceed our own), who decides what that faith must look like?

SECTION ONE:
THE RIGHTEOUS ARE JUSTIFIED BY FAITH (1:18—4:25)

Lesson Two:
Gentiles Stand Guilty Before God (1:18–32)

Paul's first major point is to highlight the need for God's justification by faith. If a person is capable of self-justification, he would not need God. Yet, human history has proved that attempts at justification by any other means—by human effort, human wisdom, idolatry, or man-made laws—have failed miserably. For a person to be justified by God, however, he must have knowledge of God's standard of justification. He must also know that *apart* from this justification, he stands condemned by Him.

Paul begins this discussion by expounding upon the consequences for those who have abandoned God's righteousness (1:18–20). He cites the Gentiles ("men") who, in past ages, have been "excluded from the commonwealth of Israel," and who had "no hope" and were "without God in the world" (Eph. 2:12). These men "knew God" (1:21) and His "ordinances" (see 1:32), but did not obey Him. These ordinances (or moral laws) pre-date the Law of Moses, extending back to "the creation of the world."

The Consequences of Unbelief (1:18–32): Someone may ask, "Just how much did the ancient people know about God anyway?"[3] The scope of this information was small in comparison to what we know today. Nonetheless, God had provided sufficient evidence in the physical creation and in man's moral nature to warrant putting one's faith in Him. Concerning a person's self-inspection, it would be clear that:

- ❏ Human beings are the highest form of life on earth.
- ❏ Human intelligence is superior to any other intelligence on earth.
- ❏ Human enterprise and creativity are superior to any other animate activity on earth.

- Humans can reason, discern, communicate, emote, and create far beyond the level of any other earthly animalistic life.
- While animals operate by instinct and (to a limited degree) learned behavior, humans operate according to a sense of justice and morality that they can temporarily circumvent but cannot remove.
- Humans have a consciousness of themselves that transcends their physical bodies; this spiritual awareness permeates every race, culture, and historical epoch ever known.
- This spiritual awareness also compels human beings to give worship to a higher being (real or imagined), as a means of validating and giving meaning to their existence.

Such qualities are evident in all people; they are meant to lead us to seek out our Creator. God has always provided a reason to believe in Him—and thus to put one's faith in Him (Heb. 11:6).

God has revealed Himself through physical nature (i.e., things that have "been made"; see Heb. 3:4), transcendent morality, and human consciousness. He has also revealed Himself through His own Presence (Gen. 18:1ff, John 12:28–30, etc.), heavenly angels (Heb. 13:2), prophets (Heb. 1:1), law (Deut. 29:29), and His own Son (Acts 17:30–31, Heb. 1:2). Regardless of how (or how much) people knew of God, Paul's point is still valid: those who deny the observable and known evidence concerning God's existence are "without excuse" (1:20).

Despite this, many have tried to suppress God's truth. To "suppress" truth does not mean merely to ignore or fail to act upon it, but to hold it down—i.e., to "prevent truth from exerting its power in the heart and the life."[4] In suppressing the truth about God, people abandon all hope of spiritual enlightenment or self-improvement. Their unconverted minds descend into animalistic desires and pleasures. What begins as moral apostasy inevitably spirals downward in deviant and self-destructive behavior (1:21–23):

- they knew God, but
- they did not honor Him, which meant
- they did not give Him thanks (i.e., were ungrateful), and thus
- they became futile (useless or vain) in their speculations—i.e., their own self-determined, mythological explanations of how they and the world came to be, etc., were unfounded, self-serving, and often absurd; thus

- their foolish heart—which was *made* foolish by having rejected the Source of its reason and intellect—was darkened, so that
- they worshiped nature (the creation of God) rather than God Himself, and images (idols) of gods of their own making.

Paganism and heathenism are not original religions of men but are themselves apostasies from the true religion of God.[5] "Darkness" (i.e., ignorance, depravity, and wickedness) indicates the absence of God's divine influence, spiritual enlightenment, and objective reality (John 3:18–21, Eph. 4:17–19). People who persistently refuse the light of God become immersed in a thick moral darkness in which they can no longer function as rational, spiritual human beings but are reduced to hedonistic, inhumane, and barbaric creatures. God's truth becomes so diluted with self-indulgence that it loses all positive influence. Such people become fixated with self-gratification at any expense, regardless of the consequences.

"Professing to be wise, they became fools" (1:22)—an ironic and profound indictment. People who turn away from God always think they are *wise* for doing so; in some cases, the idea of a divine Creator is beneath them and is cause for ridicule and scoffing. Yet, such "wisdom" is "earthly, natural, and demonic"; it creates "disorder and every evil thing" (James 3:15–16). Worshiping the *creation* rather than the *Creator* is a massive self-deception (1:23).[6]

Three times in this passage (1:24–32) we read that "God gave them over" to something far worse than that which the unconverted pagans began. As people abandon the truth of God, they also abandon the providential restraints that keep them from behaving like animals rather than those made in God's image. This moral abandonment always leads to sexual immorality and sexual deviancy, which are sins against one's own body as well as God Himself (1 Cor. 6:16–18). Thus, we see a typical digression:

- people sin against God by means of idolatry (of any kind), leading to
- sins against one's own body, which leads to and often involves (in mutual fornication)
- sins against one's fellow man.

"Natural functions" in this context refers to sexual identity and relationships that God established in the Creation (i.e., the natural order of things).

"Unnatural" means that which God never intended; defiance against the natural order; corruptions of the image of God. It is immoral for a man to "burn" with passion toward or have sex with another man because this desecrates the natural order and defies the One who created it.[7] Such perverse mating creates an unholy union; such unions incur God's wrath and punishment.[8] The only sexual union that God established in the beginning is between a man and a woman within the context of marriage (Gen. 2:24; see 1 Cor. 7:2).

Having defiled themselves, those who abandon God then defile all those around them (1:28–32). "Depraved" (1:28) means unfit, rejected (by God), or reprobate: in having rejected God, men are rejected by God.[9] In this divine rejection, such men are "given" or "handed over" to pursue their rotten vice.[10] They are "filled with" (1:29) all sorts of godless and self-serving behaviors, all of which seek personal advancement or pleasure at the expense of someone else—and their own souls.

Most of the crimes Paul lists here (1:29–31) are self-evident; many of them are closely related; similar lists of vices are found in Gal. 5:19–21 and 2 Tim. 3:1–7. This paints a truly awful picture of human depravity. When people reject God's revelation, they have no refinement or inducement to do what is good (Eph. 4:17–19, 2 Thess. 2:10–12). Chronic resistance, suppression, and sheer defiance of the truth never leads one to enlightenment; instead, such people descend further and deeper into moral darkness.[11] Even though such men "know the ordinance [law] of God," they do not care about God or His laws (1:32). In fact, they applaud and give full support to those who are like them (1 John 4:5).

Questions

1.) Are we today "without excuse" if we refuse to recognize God's existence and His authority (1:18–20)? Do we have even more evidence than what the ancients had—and if so, what might this evidence be? (Consider John 15:22 and Acts 17:30–31.)

2.) In the case of one's chronic rejection of God, moral darkness begins taking on a life of its own, dragging that person deeper and deeper into it (1:18–32).

   a. Is the depraved person responsible for his own depravity, or is this something imposed upon him through factors beyond his control?

   b. What about the *righteous* person: is righteousness imposed upon him or does he become "righteous" through factors beyond his control?

   c. Put another way: do people became callously *sinful* or honorably *righteous* because of their own decisions, or do they have no control over their behavior?

3.) Today, homosexuality is portrayed as a positive, loving, and completely normal lifestyle. Yet, Paul describes this behavior as an impurity, a dishonor based on a lie, degrading, unnatural, indecent, deserving of penalty (punishment), and depraved (1:24–28).[12]

   a. Is there any way to reconcile what Paul said with the modern narrative, or are Christians—and all people—forced to choose one over the other?

   b. Once society normalizes one "unnatural" behavior, are others sure to follow? If not, why not? If so, what would be the reason for this?

Lesson Three:
God Is an Impartial Judge (2:1–16)

God did not justify the ancient people because of their own good behavior; some other means of justification was necessary. Having abandoned the guidance of divine law, men descended into satanic wickedness of every kind. God "gave them over" to their lawless desires to the point that they became animalistic in nature.

Now Paul turns to the Jewish people. The "you" here (in 2:1) is meant most generally, as referring to any person. The ancient Gentiles were a spiritually ignorant, morally deficient, and idolatrous people, to be sure. But the Jews, taken as a whole, were hardly better. Jesus called them "an evil and adulterous generation" (Mat. 12:39), a "brood of vipers" (Mat. 12:34), worshipers of money (Luke 16:14), and condescending toward sinners (Luke 18:9). The Jews were quick to "judge" (condemn) the Gentiles' sins, yet they had many of their own sins. God would not judge only the Gentiles' sins, but the Jews' sins as well (2:2–3).

In any case, the expected response to God's revealed law—however that law is expressed—is repentance and obedience (2:4). One's stubborn resistance to God's kindness, mercy, and patience is inexcusable. God's kindness is not extended without purpose; it is designed to elicit a proper response from the one to whom it is shown (2 Peter 3:9). The Jews had far more privilege to learn of God than did the Gentiles, and with privilege comes responsibility (Luke 12: 47–48). Yet, while many Jews (and possibly even Gentile moralists) condemned the pagans and heathens, they were guilty of their own crimes—in some cases, even the same crimes as those whom they condemned. Therefore, they had "no excuse" for their crimes, just as the ancient Gentiles were also "without excuse" (recall 1:20).

God Is an Impartial Judge (2:5–11): Regarding salvation or condemnation, God is fair and impartial to all people, regardless of their nationality or ethnicity (2:5–11).[13] He judges every person according to a just and equitable standard, one which is known to those who are being judged by it. The outcome of such judgment will be dependent upon each person's response to "the truth" (2:7–8). This response must be demonstrated in his "deeds": repentance and obedience are never reduced to mere decisions but must be supported by visible and measurable actions.

"There is no partiality with God" (2:11)—God does not spare Jews or condemn Gentiles simply because of who they are. Rather, He looks at the heart of each person—what he knows, what he does, and what his intentions are (Heb. 4:12–13)—and judges accordingly. Being a just and impartial Judge, God will take into consideration in all relevant factors (upbringing, education, influences, talents, limitations, etc.) regarding one's earthly situation.

Paul speaks directly and forcefully about God's "wrath" (2:5, 8). He will direct His divine anger at those who suppress His revealed truth (recall 1:18); who do not repent; who are "selfishly ambitious," "do not obey the truth," and "[do] evil" (2:5–9). On the other hand, those who persevere in "doing good" and seek "honor and immortality" through divine grace will fully experience God's glory and honor (2:7, 10).

Law Is a Moral Standard (2:12–16): For 1,500 years, the Law of Moses governed the Jews; Gentiles were under a different law (2:12–16).[14] Each would be judged by whatever law they lived under. Jews either "live" (i.e., are justified) by their faithful obedience to the Law of Moses, or they will "perish" (i.e., be condemned) by their unfaithfulness to that Law (2:12). Gentiles, who are not under the Jews' Law, will nonetheless "live" or "perish" by a law which they *ought to have known*, based upon what has been "clearly seen, being understood through what has been made" (Rom. 1:20). One's *deeds*, not merely his knowledge (of law), reveals his true obedience or disobedience (2:13).

"Law" and "conscience" really are two different things (2:14–15). "Law" refers to the (knowledge of the) commandments themselves, while "conscience" refers to the moral governance that tells a person whether he is living in compliance with those commandments. "When the mind is at work weighing evidence and making arguments, etc., we call that 'reasoning' and when the mind renders a verdict on our conduct we call that 'conscience.' The conscience is the mind functioning as a judge!"[15] In some cases, one's conscience will accuse him of violating his knowledge of God's law; in other cases, his conscience will defend his actions as being consistent with that law. (One's conscience *can be mistaken* but still attempts to justify his behavior.) Regarding this "law" by which the Gentiles are judged:

- The Gentiles most certainly lived under a universal moral law. This law not only had to have been *known* to them, but they also had to make a conscious decision either to obey or disobey it. God cannot charge people with sin in the absence of law (Rom. 4:15, 5:13). This moral law is universal because it applies to *all* people, regardless of covenant status.
- This universal moral law was a binding requirement upon the ancients, regardless of whether it was codified (i.e., written out).
- God's divine nature serves as this universal moral law. Once a person sins against this law, he can only be justified by faith in God, no longer by obedience to law.
- All covenants made by God, whether with Jews or Gentiles, require the same *moral* laws, and thus the same moral conduct. Morality is a constant: rites, rituals, ceremonies, specific expectations, etc. may change between covenants, but morality itself never changes.
- The only covenant of salvation offered to people today is the gospel of Christ (John 14:6, Acts 4:12, 1 Tim. 2:3–6, etc.). This means that all those (of an accountable age) who are outside of Christ are judged by the universal moral law; all those who are "in Christ" are judged by the law of Christ. The *moral expectations* of both groups are the same, but those who are "in Christ" have far more responsibilities because of their covenant relationship with God.
- One who is outside of Christ—an unconverted sinner—is not bound to the gospel of Christ but to the universal moral law. A person cannot be bound to a covenant to which he never agreed to honor. Once a person is baptized into Christ, however, he agrees to the covenant terms and is bound to this covenant for the rest of his life.

Paul's emphasis is that God is a fair and impartial Judge; therefore, He can justify the one who puts his faith in Him, regardless of what law he is under. God would be unfair and partial, however, if He judged a person according to a standard (law or covenant) that was unknown or did not apply to him.[16] "[A]ccording to my gospel" (2:16) does *not* mean that every man will be judged *by* the gospel, but that Paul's gospel spells out the state of being of every person, whether he is in Christ or not.[17] Even so, *all* judgment will be conducted "through Christ Jesus" (see John 5:22–30 and 2 Cor. 5:10). Just as all salvation comes through Christ, so all judgment comes through Him.

Questions

1.) What exactly is "repentance" (2:4)? Is this a person's *only* appropriate response to God's kindness and patience, or are there other necessary responses as well? If other responses are required as well, why does Paul focus on repentance in this passage?

2.) Our personal biases, favoritism (of those whom we love), and limited knowledge often compromises our human judgment of other people. How does God overcome these human flaws to be an impartial judge (2:9–11)?

3.) Will a person stand justified before God if his conscience does not "accuse" him of any crimes (2:14–15)? Is conscience alone a sufficient means of justification? (Compare Acts 23:1 and 1 Tim. 1:12–13; see also 1 Cor. 4:3–4.)

Lesson Four:
Jews Also Stand Guilty Before God
(2:17–29)

All implications aside, Paul now speaks to Jews in a broad, historical sense. Specifically, he has in mind those who "rely upon the Law [of Moses] and boast in [their covenant relationship with] God" (2:1, bracketed words are mine). These are not Jewish Christians but are Jews who put their confidence in law-keeping as a means of righteousness (see Rom. 10:2–4). Thus, "you" must refer to the Jews generally and not to members of the church in Rome—most of whom he does not even know.

The Jews Are Also Lawbreakers (2:17–24): Paul does not deny the enlightenment a Jew might offer a Gentile (2:17–20); he merely states that this privilege by itself does not translate to righteousness. The Jews were keepers and guardians of the Law of Moses—a fact they often and proudly paraded before the Gentiles—yet they could not be justified by that Law (Acts 13:38–39, 15:6–11). Their violation of the Law of Moses made them sinners just like Gentiles who violated God's moral law (2:21–23).

Specifically, some Jews were guilty of theft (2:21), often by withholding from God what should have been given to Him (Mal. 3:8–9) or by withholding from their parents what the Law commanded (Mat. 15:4–6). Also, some Jews were guilty of adultery (2:22)—Jesus Himself called them "an evil and adulterous generation" (Mat. 12:39)—if not against their spouses, then against their covenant with God. And, while the Jews did not practice idolatry in the way that their forefathers did, they "robbed temples" [lit., committed sacrilege against holy things (of God)], again by withholding tithes and sacrifices from God, or by using temple donations for ungodly purposes.

In other words, the Jews boasted in being law-keepers when in fact (historically) they were lawbreakers, putting them in league with the Gentiles who did the same thing. Instead of humbling their hearts and repenting (recall 2:4), thus setting an excellent example for the Gentiles to follow, they blasphemed (profaned) God's name in their arrogance (2:24). Paul quotes from Isa. 52:5 to underscore this—in other words, this is not a new problem but a deeply entrenched one.

Circumcision of the Heart (2:25–29): The Jews also boasted in their circumcision [lit., cutting off the male foreskin], since this was distinctive of their covenant with God (Gen. 17:10–11, Lev. 12:1–3, etc.). Yet, Paul responds that their unfaithfulness to that covenant rendered their physical circumcision useless. In fact, the uncircumcised Gentile could be justified by his faith *without* circumcision. In other words, circumcision (which often was used to symbolize obedience to the entire Law) was not the source of righteousness but *faith*.

The Jew might be one "outwardly" because of his ethnicity, heritage, and physical conformity to the Law, but the Gentile's inward faith was what God sought all along (2:28).[18] True circumcision "is that which is of the heart, by the Spirit, not by the letter [of the Law]" (2:25–29). The Jews put great emphasis on the flesh; God's emphasis in on the human heart (Col. 2:11–12).[19] So it is today: true Christianity is not about religious rites and churchgoing but genuine faith in God for salvation. Some Christians miss the point: they put emphasis on their works but not enough attention on the condition of their heart.

What Paul is really saying—and this reverberates throughout the entire epistle—is this: God has *always* justified people "by faith," not law-keeping. And inseparable from this, God has *always* justified people through divine grace (as a response to human faith), not law-keeping. No one can keep the laws of God perfectly, save Jesus Christ, so the only recourse the sinner has is "by grace … through faith" (Eph. 2:8). Faith is not a new subject that Paul introduces to the world but an ongoing one. The only thing that has changed from ancient times is that *Christ* now needs to be the object of one's faith.

Questions

1.) Jewish leaders, particularly in Christ's day, considered themselves superior to the common Jews because of their knowledge of the Law (see Mat. 23:1–3 and John 7:49).

   a. Will God justify any person based on his knowledge alone?

   b. Can one be knowledgeable about God yet fail to live by faith in Him?

2.) Is the gospel of Christ "blasphemed" or "dishonored" (2:24) among those who claim to believe in it but deliberately refuse to keep it? Please explain.

3.) Paul wrote, "He is not a Jew who is one outwardly … who is one inwardly" (2:28–29). If we replace "Jew" with "Christian," does this statement still make sense?

   a. Does Paul mean, "It doesn't matter what you *believe*, as long as your heart is right before God"?

   b. Does Paul mean, "It doesn't matter what you *do* (or do *not* do), as long as your heart is right before God"?

Lesson Five:
All Have Sinned and
Are Guilty Before God (3:1–20)

Paul has thus far made some extremely controversial statements, especially from a Jewish point-of-view. It might seem, then, that he favors Gentiles over Jews, or that he is justifying salvation to Gentiles at the Jews' expense. Anticipating these objections, Paul provides several rhetorical statements (both literal and implied) to clarify the position upon which he is expounding (3:1–8).

> **First:** "If a Jew is no better than a Gentile, what benefit is it to be a Jew?" (paraphrase of 3:1). Yet, Paul says, the Jew *does* have an advantage over the Gentile (3:2)—even though this advantage will not by itself *save* him. This also provides a springboard into the next point, namely, that God is faithful to the "oracles" which He entrusted to Israel.

> **Second:** "If some [Jews] did not believe, their unbelief will not nullify the faithfulness of God, will it?" (paraphrase of 3:3). Paul's point: the oracles (promises) of God concerning universal salvation were not dependent upon the faithfulness of the entire nation of Israel. Even as He sent the people of Israel into captivity for their sins, God remained faithful to His covenant with them (Lev. 26:40–45). The promises He makes to one person are not nullified by the faithlessness of another. Even if every person were a liar, God will never lie or default on His promises (2 Tim. 2:13, Titus 1:2).

> **Third:** "If God is shown to be faithful despite men's unfaithfulness, then why is God angry with men—especially the Jews?" (paraphrase of 3:5). Paul anticipates a Jew proposing the following conundrum: "Although we [Jews] put the Messiah to death, this is exactly what God wanted and expected us to do for the benefit of all humankind. How then can He find fault with us?"[20] This would be like God thanking the serpent for deceiving Adam and Eve so that Christ could offer His gospel of salvation! The gift of grace is never a license to sin, nor does it condone sinning to bring about more grace.

Fourth: "If the gospel glorifies God by highlighting the disobedience of men, then is God fair to condemn men whose sins actually magnify God's grace?" (paraphrase of 3:7). The reality is just the opposite: one's sin dishonors God (recall 2:24), so that the result (saving grace) does not justify the means (human sin). Furthermore, God is glorified only when sinners choose obedience over disobedience, not the other way around.

Fifth: "If sin glorifies God, then let us sin often!" (paraphrase of 3:8). This maligns what Paul preached, yet he some accused him of saying it. God never endorses (directly or indirectly) those who act irresponsibly or immorally. Thus, Paul is blunt in his response: "Their condemnation is just."

All People Are Guilty before God (3:9–20): "What then? Are we [Jews] better than they [Gentiles]? Not at all…" (3:9). Paul now brings his argument to a climax (3:9–18): *all* who have sinned against *any* law of God are sinners, whether Gentiles (learned Greeks or barbaric heathens) or Jews (including ancient Israelites). God is faithful to all men—thus innocent of any injustice or sin—but all people have failed in every attempt at self-justification.

Pulling together several OT quotes,[21] Paul paints a grim picture: despite great human accomplishments otherwise, all people are (morally and spiritually) fallen creatures. No person can remove the guilt of his sin or the damage it causes. "There is none righteous, not even one" (3:10)—this refers to a person's state of being apart from having been justified by God for his faith in God. Where Paul is leading with this discussion is clear: since all have sinned, therefore all need the grace of God. And grace will not work in the absence of human faith.

The Law of Moses was never meant to redeem sinners; it could not restore one's lost innocence before God (3:19–20). Cold, unsympathetic, and inflexible law cannot save the one who sins against it. The only thing law can do is to justify the one who keeps it perfectly *or* condemn the one who violates it. "Every mouth [is] closed [lit., silenced; stopped[22]]" means that no person has a right to speak in his defense, since every person stands guilty before God (see Rom. 11:32 and Gal. 3:22 for similar usage).

Since God is our Creator, and we are His Creation, "all the world" is accountable to Him. He has sovereign authority over us; we must answer to that authority. He is the lawgiver—and we are all law-*breakers*—and He must enforce His law. Furthermore, "through the Law [or, through law] comes the knowledge of sin" (3:20): God has provided a code of righteousness, and anything that falls short of this is sin (Rom. 7:7–12, Gal. 3:19, etc.). Thus, we know (through His law) what both righteousness *and* sin look like.

Questions

1.) Do people still try to rationalize their sins today? Can one's clever argument excuse him of guilt or condemnation before God? Please explain.

2.) If Christ's gospel rested upon the obedience of mere men, what would this say about the strength of that gospel, or our confidence in it?

   a. Are there religions today that rest upon the merits of their founders or other mere men? Can these save the souls of those who believe in them?

   b. Regardless, might some Christians rest their faith upon the merits or faithfulness of others (including spouses, mentors, preachers, and friends) rather than putting their full confidence in Christ?

3.) To deal appropriately with sin, we (sinners) must take responsibility for our own sins. In other words, before rushing to the *solution*, how are we to understand the *problem* (3:1–20)?

Lesson Six:
We Are Justified by Grace through Faith (3:21–31)

Justification by Faith, Not Law (3:23–31): Human sin is the problem and Jesus Christ is the solution (3:21–26). While our sins separate us from God, Christ can reconcile us with God through Himself—that is, through His own worthiness. God's righteousness is revealed *not* simply by the giving of law, but more importantly by providing a way of escape from law's condemnation (3:21–22).[23] (The "apart from law" phrase will be addressed shortly.)

"[F]or all have sinned…" (3:23): every person who is accountable to God's law eventually *breaks* it, incurring his own guilt. To "fall short of the glory [lit., holiness] of God" means to fail in one's moral obligation to keep what the Creator has established as a code of righteousness (i.e., God's holy nature).[24] The only way a sinner can be justified [lit., made innocent] before God is through His saving grace which comes by way of the blood of Christ. This grace is a "gift" because: it is undeserved; it is unearned; it cannot be purchased; it cannot be obtained through any other means.[25]

God imparts grace to "all those who believe" (3:22)—regardless of Jew or Gentile—through the blood of Christ (3:24–25). As a result of His sacrificial death on the cross, Christ redeems the believer's soul from law's condemnation (3:25). His blood provides "propitiation," meaning, the appeasement of God's wrath for our having sinned against Him. In this way He becomes the sinner's Advocate, and His blood cleanses the contrite sinner of his guilt (1 John 1:7, 9, and 2:1–2).[26]

Christ's sacrifice on the cross covers (atones for) all sins committed *prior* to it as well as all sins committed *after* it.[27] His death not only fulfilled the blood offerings of the Law of Moses, but also satisfied "once for all" what God required of the sinner (Heb. 5:9): that person's life. Blood is the essence of life (Lev. 17:10–11), the physical substance that links a person to his spiritual (non-physical) existence. Christ's literal and uncorrupted blood necessarily required a literal and uncorrupted body (Heb. 10:5–10). We are justified, then, by His body *and* His blood, for one is impossible without the other.

Paul's point: God is both *just* (or, righteous toward men) and the *justifier* (the determiner of the righteousness *of* men) (3:26). God never credits righteousness *apart* from one's faith but only when one *lives* by faith. This need for divine grace nullifies all human boasting—in oneself, his law-keeping, or self-justification (3:27). One cannot boast in the very law he has broken, since that law can no longer justify him. Now he must depend upon something *apart* from law.

A "law of faith" (3:27) means here a law that *defines what this faith must look like*, rather than each one defining "faith" on his own. If God justifies us by faith in Him, He also has the right and responsibility to reveal what this faith must be. We are thus "justified by faith apart from works of the Law" (3:28).[28] The means of justification of the human soul lies outside of human effort, human works, or human ability. The best we can do is to keep the law of God; but once we fail—even once (James 2:10)—we are fully dependent upon *divine grace* to restore us to innocence. This is what "apart from" law means. Law can only describe the situation at hand; it cannot make innocent the lawbreaker. Divine grace *can* and *does* restore the human soul, but this is conditioned upon one's obedient faith. God's system of grace-through-faith functions equally with both Jew and Gentile (3:29–30). He does not justify one differently than He justifies the other (Rom. 10:12).

Paul then anticipates another objection, likely from a Jew (3:31), which we might paraphrase: "Does the teaching of the gospel to Gentiles nullify the Law of Moses given to the Jews?" Put another way: "Does being justified by faith nullify the need for law?" Paul responds confidently: "May it never be!" No one can live in fellowship with God who will not keep His laws (1 John 2:4–6). Since justification by faith preceded the Law of Moses, then it makes sense that the Law cannot be in contradiction to this justification.

"On the contrary, we establish the Law" (3:31)—lit., "we establish law," since there is no definite article ("the") before either use of "law" in this verse. The binding force of God's universal moral code of expected human behavior is upheld if, having violated that law, we must be justified by faith. In other words, the fact that we need faith in God underscores the fact that we have sinned against a law that most certainly *does exist* (because we cannot sin against a law that does *not* exist). In this way, "we establish [support; honor the standing of]" the existence of divine law. If we were not lawbreakers, then neither would we need faith, grace, or justification.

Questions

1.) The fact that *all* have sinned (and fallen) and God *justifies* all through faith puts all people on equal footing, whether we are sinners or saints (3:23–24).

   a. How should this affect our attitude toward those who remain lost?

   b. How does this make seeking human approval a useless pursuit?

2.) In classical Greek, "propitiation" (3:25) referred to sacrifices made to pagan gods to acquire blessings from them (in the form of crops, herds, or children), to secure an advantage over their enemies, and/or to keep those gods from destroying those who worshiped them.

   a. In the case of a Christian, who provided the sacrifice for his propitiation—and why is this important? (Consider Heb. 2:17 and 1 John 2:1–2 in your answer.)

   b. Is God seeking to destroy us or to save us? (Consider John 4:23, Eph. 2:4–5, 1 Thess. 5:9–10, and 1 Tim. 2:3–6 in your answer.)

3.) Law-keeping involves measurable, quantifiable results rather than something as seemingly abstract as "faith." Therefore, people often seek to be justified by what they *do* rather than the One in whom they *believe*.

   a. Given this, why is it easier to boast in *what* one does rather than in the One who *approves* of what he does? How can we avoid such boasting?

   b. Does one's human effort (in keeping God's laws) no longer count for anything, if he is justified by faith? Is faith itself measurable?

Lesson Seven: Historical Examples of Justification by Faith (4:1–25)

Works Cannot Save Sinners (4:1–8): No person—save Christ—can be justified by law, since all fall short of the glory of God (recall 3:23). As a case in point, Paul cites one of the most respected men of all time (Abraham) to show that he was justified by faith, not perfect law-keeping (4:1–12; see Heb. 11:8–19). Abraham serves as an ideal representative here since he was the forefather of Gentiles (through Ishmael) as well as Jews (through Isaac).

God "reckoned" or credited righteousness to Abraham because of his belief in Him, even though he had not yet seen what God had promised him (Gen. 15:6). If he had been sinless, then he would have received his righteousness as earned "wages" (4:4) rather than having it bestowed upon him as a gift. As it was, Abraham was not a perfect man and thus required God's intervention (grace) based upon the confidence (faith) he put in Him (4:2-4). This reveals a great paradox: faith must have works to make it real, yet no one is justified *by* those works. A person's "faith [in God] is credited as righteousness [by God]" (4:5) once that faith is made real through appropriate action.

Paul then introduces another man whom the Jews greatly respected (4:6–8): King David. David's sins are well-documented in Scripture; yet God forgave him of those sins. This forgiveness was imparted because of God's grace as the result of David's faith in Him. It was "apart from works" (4:6) in the sense that such forgiveness could not be achieved through law-keeping (or human effort): David's sins made this impossible. Divine action is required for a person to be forgiven (4:7–8; Paul quotes from Psalm 32:1–2), but such action requires that a person demonstrate his faith in God.

Faith Is Greater Than Circumcision (4:9–15): The Jews prided themselves on their circumcision, since this was a sign of the covenant given to them by God through Abraham (Gen. 17). Yet God credited Abraham with righteousness *before* he was circumcised; and God forgave David *regardless* of it (4:9–12; see John 8:39). The system of justification by faith, then, precedes the Jews' boast in circumcision and is therefore superior to it. "Circumcision is nothing, and uncircumcision is nothing, but what matters is the keeping of the commandments of God" (1 Cor. 7:19). Believers demonstrate faith by keeping God's commandments (1 John 5:1–4), and without faith it is impossible to have fellowship with God (Heb. 11:6).

The divine promise of blessing and salvation to "all the families of the earth" (Gen. 12:1–3) would be "nullified" (i.e., rendered useless) if it had been dependent upon every Jew's perfect law-keeping (4:14). Instead, it rests upon God's divine ability as demonstrated through Christ. Law "brings about wrath" to those who disobey it (4:15); such wrath implies impending punishment. If there was no law of God, there would be no standard by which to judge human behavior; one cannot be in violation of a law that does not exist (4:15).

Just as Abraham was justified by grace through his faith in God, so is every person today justified the same way (4:16; see Gal. 3:18 and Eph. 2:8). When we exhibit the same faith as Abraham, "the father of us all [who believe]," we become his descendants and are heirs of the divine promise (Rom. 9:8, Gal. 3:7, 29). This is implied in God's having changed Abram's name to "Abraham," meaning, "a father of many nations" (4:17a, quoted from Gen. 17:5). We are not his descendants according to a physical lineage but a living faith.

Paul includes an example of the kind of faith that Abraham demonstrated (4:17b–21; see Gen. 17:15–19 and 18:1–14). Abraham was an old man (one hundred years) and Sarah, his wife, was an old woman (ninety years). Sarah's womb was, in a sense, doubly-dead: it was both barren and beyond child-bearing years. Yet, God promised Abraham a son through his wife, and Abraham believed that God could "[call] into being that which does not exist" (4:17b). Thus, he believed "in hope against hope" (4:18)—that is, in hope *in the divine promise* against all hope *in human ability*. He put his future entirely in God's hands and believed that He was able to perform where all human effort would fail (4:21).

The record of Abraham's faith serves as a model example for the kind of faith God expects of us (4:23–25). First, one must believe that God is willing and able to perform beyond any human or natural effort. Second, one must demonstrate that faith in some visible and measurable way. Specifically, one must believe that Jesus resurrected from the dead and then live according to that belief (4:24). Just as Abraham's own ability to fulfill God's promise was "dead" (Heb. 11:11–12), so we are "dead" to God without Christ (Eph. 2:1).

Questions

1.) Is "belief" by itself a work of faith (see John 6:29)? If so, then is it enough merely to believe in God to be saved—and is this what is meant in 4:3? If not, then why *must* we believe to be saved (Acts 16:30–31)?

2.) Righteousness is a gift, not compensation for work performed (4:4). If God merely compensated us for good works, this would invalidate the need for His grace.

   a. What compensation (wages) *do* we earn once we have sinned against God (see 6:23)? Why is it critically important that we realize this?

   b. Even so, Christians sometimes justify themselves by (or rest their salvation on) pious living, Bible knowledge, church work, preaching, etc. Why do you suppose they do this? Should they stop doing these things altogether?

3.) Paul says we are justified by faith "apart from works" (4:6); James says we are justified by works, and that "faith without works is dead" (James 2:20–24). Conspicuously, both men cite Abraham to underscore their point.

   a. How are we to reconcile both positions? Are these positions in conflict with each other or are both men looking at the same thing from different vantage points?

   b. Will God impart saving grace to anyone who has not (for any reason) shown obedient faith in Him? If so, what is the point of *having* faith? If not, then are works required to *demonstrate* an obedient faith?

Section Two: Benefits of Being Justified by Faith (5:1—8:39)

Lesson Eight: The Benefit of Peace with God (5:1–21)

Now Paul takes justification by faith to another level. Not only is the faithful believer credited with righteousness, but he also receives tremendous spiritual benefits. These benefits include peace with God (chapter 5); newness of life (chapter 6); freedom from condemnation (chapter 7); and the indwelling of the Holy Spirit (chapter 8).

Christ's Intercession for Sinners (5:1–11): "Therefore" (5:1) indicates that the conclusions Paul is about to draw build upon the foundation already laid in previous chapters. Notice the order (sequence) of the giving of these benefits (5:1–2):

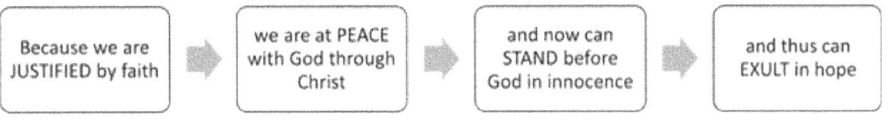

Faith is the catalyst for God's justification: no one can seek His favor without it. Both faith and justification are objective in nature: faith needs to be *in* someone, and "justification" requires someone to *do* the justifying. The object of our faith is Jesus Christ (recall 3:23–26): He is the One in whom we must place our faith. The justifier is God, the only One in the position and having the authority to do this.

"Peace with God" is a real condition of the soul, not a mere sensation of the human conscience. To be at peace with God requires unity with Him, which is only possible through His grace. This grace is possible only through the redemptive and intercessory work of "our Lord Jesus Christ" (5:1). The Greek word for "introduction" (5:2) is also translated "access" (Eph. 2:18, 3:12): we have access to God when we live by faith in Him, but we stand before God because of His grace. All of this is cause for exultation—i.e., glorying or boasting in God because of what He has done for the one who believes in Him (1 Cor. 1:30–31).

Those who are at peace with God can overcome this world (5:3–5). Paul explains the process of this overcoming:

- **"we exult in our tribulations"**: This does not mean we are happy to endure these, but—having been justified—we can see their positive effect on our spiritual well-being (James 1:2–4).[29] While the unconverted suffer without hope, believers suffer with a view to their redemption. Thus, we have peace amid tribulation, hope amid suffering, and can "exult" (or boast; rejoice) because of our spiritual standing with God.
- **"… perseverance"**: This refers to the tenacity and determination to keep on keeping on, despite discouragements and struggles (Heb. 10:36).
- **"… proven character"**: This refers to a "tried condition" in which something (or someone) is put to the test.[30] God allows (and provides opportunities) for our faith to be "tested," since an untested faith really is no faith at all (1 Peter 1:6–9).
- **"… hope"**: The Christian's hope is based upon the authority of Jesus Christ and His proven worthiness (2 Tim. 2:11–13). The Holy Spirit is "given to us"—the context here has nothing to do with miracles (as in Acts 8:14–17) but what is done for every person in whom the love of God has been "poured out," resulting in salvation (recall 8:6–9).

Paul then emphasizes how great our justification really is by magnifying what God did to secure it. This passage (5:6–11) is one of the finest summations of the gospel of Christ in the NT. First, Paul reveals the awful situation of those condemned because of sin. They are:

- **"helpless" (5:6)** to save themselves.
- **"ungodly" (5:6)** because they are separated from God (Isa. 59:1–2, Eph. 2:1–3).
- **"sinners" (5:8)** because they practice sin (1 John 3:4–10), regardless of the kind, quantity, or frequency of those sins.
- **under divine wrath (5:9)** because they stand condemned by God.
- **"enemies" (5:10)** because whoever befriends the godless world takes on that world's hostile character and therefore stands opposed to God (James 4:4).

This paints a bleak and frightening picture. Those who are outside of Christ (i.e., not "in Christ") are in a realm of spiritual darkness from which they cannot escape; this is what it means to be "lost" (as in Luke 15:24, 19:10). While still on earth, sinners do not experience the full effect of what this means; often, they are altogether oblivious to their problem. While a person remains alive *there is hope*, but his hope is only in Jesus Christ. God sent His Son to save us from our horrible predicament "at the right time" (5:6). Christ died "when the fullness of the time" came (Gal. 4:4) and only God could know what and when this "fullness" would be.

"Christ died for the ungodly" (5:6)—while "sinners" incur a death sentence, Christ provides *His* death as a satisfaction of (or propitiation for) this sentence (1 Peter 2:24). While someone might die for what that person believes is a "good man," Christ died for an untold number of *very bad people*—all enemies of God (5:7–8). The fact that He was willing to save us when we were at our worst magnifies His great love for us.

Christ's blood serves as the physical agent of atonement by which we are "justified" (5:9). He offered His "once for all" sacrifice to cleanse the soul of every person who calls upon the name of the Lord for salvation. The ancient Israelites offered animal sacrifices in faith, but animal blood could never remove sins (Heb. 10:1–10). Yet, every believer *is* justified (made innocent) through the blood of Christ (Eph. 1:7). Blood represents life (Lev. 17:10–11): in having been justified by Christ's blood, we are in fact justified by His *life* (1 Peter 3:18).

God brings us into His fellowship through Christ (5:10). "Reconciliation" means "being made friends with again"—and thus no longer enemies.[31] This necessarily implies a previous good standing: one cannot be reconciled to a stranger, or to one from whom he has never been severed.[32] Since Jesus is no longer dead but now reigns as our High Priest (Heb. 8:1), we are saved not only through His death but especially through His resurrected life, since He now mediates for us (5:10; see 1 Tim. 2:4–5 and Heb. 4:14–16).

Contrast of Christ's Gift and Adam's Fall (5:12–21): This section is admittedly difficult, partly because of the erroneous religious teaching that has been based upon it—namely, the so-called Doctrine of Original Sin—and partly because of the complex grammatical construction.[33] It helps to clarify the passage if one regards 5:13–17 as a parenthetical statement (which it is) and then reads 5:18 immediately following 5:12, as you see below:

> Therefore, just as through one man sin entered into the world, and death through sin, and so death spread to all men, because all sinned (. . .), so then as through one transgression there resulted condemnation to all men, even so through one act of righteousness there resulted justification of life to all men.

"Adam" refers to the man himself, the ancestor of all humanity (5:12; see Gen. 5:1–2). Though it was Eve who sinned first (Gen. 3:1–6, 1 Tim. 2:14), it was Adam who bears the ultimate responsibility for bringing sin into the family, so to speak. His sin affects all those who come after him—thus, the entire human race. Through the very first human, "sin entered the world" and "death" was the curse for this (Gen. 2:16–17, Rom. 6:23, etc.). Consequentially, "death spread to all men" in a twofold sense:

- **First:** since the entire family of man is under a curse, all who are in that family will suffer its effects. To clarify: all will suffer the *effects* or *consequences* of sin in the world, but *guilt* is a far different matter. Each person bears his own guilt when he sins against God: "...*because all sinned*" (5:12, emphasis added). This is not a new thought: "Fathers shall not be put to death for their sons, nor shall sons be put to death for their fathers; *everyone shall be put to death for his own sin*" (Deut. 24:16, emphasis added; see also Ezek. 18:20).
- **Second:** since sin is in the family (of man), each member of the family has the propensity or inclination to sin—and thus *will* sin eventually.[34] Adam's personal sin representatively communicates what will happen to all his posterity in due time, even if we do not commit the exact same error that he did.

In a parenthetical excursion from the thought he just began, Paul takes a moment to clarify some things (5:13–17):

- "sin was in the world" even before the Law of Moses defined, codified, and magnified its presence. If Adam (who lived long before the Law) was guilty of sin, he must have been under a law (5:13).
- "from Adam until Moses" humankind still sinned against God and suffered under the curse of sin (5:14).
- "free gift" (5:15–17) recalls 3:24: "[We are] justified as a gift by His grace through the redemption which is in Christ Jesus." The "gift" is God's saving grace, which is personified in Christ Himself (Titus 2:11, 3:4–5). "But the free gift [of God] is not like the transgression [of Adam]"—in several ways:

Adam's Transgressions	Christ's "Free Gift"
came through a man	came through the Son of God
was the result of temptation	was the result of perfect obedience
incurred divine condemnation	provides divine forgiveness
many "died" (were cursed)	many live (the curse is overcome)[35]
many live (the curse is overcome)	leads to justification
many are made sinners (when they sin, following in the footsteps of Adam)	many are made righteous (when they believe in God, following in the footsteps of Christ)

Since death is the payment (wage) for sin (Rom. 6:23), the effect of sin is not a "gift" but a horrible consequence (5:15). Grace, however, is not a "consequence" of faith but is gifted to those who seek God's fellowship. Sin only brings death and nothing else, but Christ brings a life overflowing with manifold blessings and advantages. In other words, it is not simply an exchange of "life" for "death."

❑ In 5:16, Paul inverts the effects of one man (Adam) against the other (Christ). In Adam's case, *one sin* led to "many transgressions"; in Christ, these many transgressions are removed through the righteousness of *one life* (Christ's). While Adam's sin began a chain of events that negatively affected all human history, Christ's righteous life breaks that chain and gives fellowship with God in the place of condemnation.[36]

Paul picks up in 5:18 where he left off in 5:12 and continues to show the contrasts between the "first" Adam and the "second" Adam (Christ; see 1 Cor. 15:22). "The Law came in so that the transgression would increase" (5:20): God's laws magnify not only how sinful people really are but also how holy God is—and how sin severs people from God's holy fellowship. Law also magnifies the desperate human need for divine help in restoration to God's fellowship. The more people sin, the more they need God's saving grace; "where sin increased, grace abounded all the more" (5:20).

Questions

1.) What certain conditions must exist for one to have "peace with God" (5:1–2)?

2.) Paul says that "at the right time Christ died for the ungodly" (5:6). What does this tell us about the way in which God operates? Might "time" here also imply *timing*?

3.) Since Christ died for us "while we were yet sinners" (5:6–8), what does this say about the genuineness and selflessness of His intentions? What is He willing to do for us once we become His friends (consider John 15:12–17)?

4.) What does Christ have in common with Adam? What are the contrasts between the two? Why is it important that we see Christ as a likeness of Adam, but without Adam's limited or inferior characteristics?

Lesson Nine:
The Benefit of Newness of Life (6:1–23)

In response to what he just said, Paul anticipates someone thinking that the abundance of saving grace will encourage the practice of sin (6:1). This reasoning, of course, is illogical: God never promotes evil to bring about good. The practice of sin is incompatible with the practice of righteousness (1 John 3:4-10). Thus, Paul's strong response: "May it never be!" (6:2a).

One who has died to his allegiance to sin cannot still put himself under sin's control (6:2b). Death severs one's allegiance to his master, regardless of whether it is the death of the master or that of the servant (as in the sinner's case). The action that symbolizes our death to sin's reign (recall 5:21) and our new allegiance to Christ is baptism—immersion in water (6:3).[37] In other words, sin does not die to us, but we die to sin; sin continues to reign over other people, but (once we are baptized) Christ reigns over us.

Walking in Newness of Life (6:3-11): Baptism symbolizes one's death, burial, and resurrection to "newness of life" (6:3-4). Just because baptism is symbolic does not make it optional, expendable, or unnecessary. The Passover celebration was hugely symbolic, yet God commanded the Israelites to observe it.[38] Many denominational teachers today reject the necessity of baptism for salvation, stating that it is merely "an outward sign of an inward grace" (a teaching of Calvinism). The NT simply does not anywhere teach this, but people do.[39]

Christ died on the cross, was buried in the earth, and rose from the dead. His "old" life on earth ended (John 19:30); "behold, new things have come" (2 Cor. 5:17). Likewise, the believer also "dies" to his "old" self, is buried in a watery grave, and is resurrected to serve a new Master. The believer's actions are symbolic *of* Christ's literal death, burial, and resurrection. Both deaths are real but not equal: ours follows in form, not in significance. Nonetheless, through this act of faith, the believer:

- is baptized into Christ (i.e., His body, the church—Col. 1:18).
- is baptized into His death—i.e., he chooses what Jesus chose (2 Tim. 2:11).
- obeys Christ's command (Mat. 28:19) out of his love for Him (John

14:15).
- "[calls] upon the name of the Lord" (Acts 22:16).
- is "born again" (John 3:5, 1 Peter 1:3) or "born of God" (John 1:12-13).
- His "body of sin" is "done away with" since he submits to the God-given process to accomplish this (6:6). From this point forward, that person's allegiance is to be with Christ, no longer to sin (6:6-7).

Baptism is the visible event that marks one's spiritual transition from the world to Christ's church (Col. 1:13-14). It is the historical point of reference with which his full allegiance to Christ begins (Gal. 3:27).

The one who has died *with* Christ now belongs *to* Him (6:7). This implies a spiritual transaction: God purchases that person's soul through the blood of Christ; he no longer belongs to himself but is God's possession (1 Cor. 6:19-20, Titus 2:14). Just as he is not "partially" buried in water but fully immersed, so he is not "partially" dead to sin but fully. Having been "united with [Christ] in the likeness of His death" (6:5), "we shall also live with Him" in the likeness of His glory (6:8): first, as imitators of Him; second, in his glorified state (1 John 3:2). Just as Christ will never die again, so the believer's soul will never die; death is no longer "master" over him—it has no "victory" or "sting" as before (1 Cor. 15:54-57).

Being "freed from sin" (6:7) does not mean (and cannot mean) that the believer will never sin again. It means that once he was a servant of sin, but now he is a servant of the Lord. Salvation is always a conditional promise (*"If* we have died with Christ…"—6:8). Unless the premise is satisfied, the promise will be nullified.

As Christ died to (the world of) sin "once for all" (6:10; see Heb. 10:10, 14), so the Christian has died to sin once for all. That which "once for all" completed will never need to be done again. Thus, there is no unfinished business on God's part regarding the salvation of human souls. The subject here is not perfect or flawless obedience on our part but faithful *allegiance.* While even the most faithful Christian will still sin, he will not abandon his allegiance to Christ (see 1 John 1:5—2:2). This is what it means to be "dead to sin, but alive to God in Christ Jesus" (6:11).

A New Allegiance to a New Master (6:12-23): Having defined the process by which one is justified to God, Paul now makes practical use of this transaction (6:12-23). Since the Christian is no longer a servant of sin, the "members of your body"—i.e., one's physical body—can no longer participate in sinful action. Just as one's heart belongs to Christ, so also does his body: this must submit to the same God who has given life to his spirit. Therefore, one's body is now for the purpose of righteousness, in conformity with the One who sanctifies him (1 Thess. 4:7, 1 Peter 1:15, etc.). It is incompatible with the gospel—and one's baptism—to practice sin while claiming to be a Christian.

Paul further explains: a Christian is "not under law but under grace" (6:14)—that is, he is no longer condemned by law (as a lawbreaker) but is justified by grace through his faith in the Justifier (recall 3:26; see Eph. 2:8, Titus 3:7, etc.). Paul's words here are misrepresented by some to mean, "You no longer have to obey commandments because you are always covered by grace." Yet, God will never permit, condone, or enable sin simply because of the availability of grace (6:15; recall 6:1-2). It is impossible to remain true to the gospel of Christ by purposely avoiding any of God's commandments.

Christians—those baptized into Christ—are still servants, but to *God*, not sin (6:16-18). Servitude here necessarily implies obedience, and obedience to God is impossible apart from honoring His laws. Every person, Paul implies, serves *someone* or *something*, whether it be God or another master. Servitude to sin leads to death; servitude to God leads to righteousness (6:16).

The Roman Christians did not just stumble into obedience, servitude to God, or Christianity in general. They *learned* of these things through preachers of the gospel. Salvation is not something that happens to a person without his knowledge or consent. It is a *decision* of the believer based upon "that form of teaching" (6:17)—or "the doctrine conforming to godliness" (1 Tim. 6:3)—that he learned from God's word (see Eph. 1:13-14, Col. 1:5). This "form of teaching" necessarily implies a *revealed pattern of instruction* given by God so we can know "the will of the Lord" (Eph. 5:17).[40] One cannot be a "slave of righteousness" (6:18) who refuses—for any reason—this "form of teaching."

Paul sets the two allegiances—to sin and to God—in contrast (6:19–23):

Living under Moral Law		Living under Grace
Innocent, until a single violation of law	J u s t i f i e d by G o d	Made innocent, through the perfect obedience of Christ
Once having sinned, are condemned by God		Once having been justified, are reconciled to God
…are now slaves to sin		…are now servants of God
Disobedience continues, without any recourse		Righteousness continues as faith continues
Are unable to be righteous, but remain "sinners"		Are "freed from sin" (6:7)—i.e., no longer live as sinners
Derive no benefit from sin		Derive tremendous benefits from God's mercy and grace
"the wages of sin is death"		"the free gift of God is eternal life in Christ" (6:23)

What benefit does one derive from an allegiance to sin? Paul says bluntly: there is none. Sin is inherently destructive, corrosive, and debilitating; it produces nothing but sorrow, shame, and ruin. Those enslaved to sin are "free [as in, unaffected or uninfluenced—MY WORDS] in regard to righteousness" (6:20). "For the outcome of those things [which you used to practice—MY WORDS] is death" (6:21): while the NT does not use the phrase "spiritual death," this is what is meant here. This does not refer to a soul's annihilation—a teaching foreign to the NT—but a permanent separation from God (Eph. 2:1-3).

"But now…" (6:22)—for the one who is "in Christ," *things have been radically and indescribably improved.* Instead of an eternal death (separation from God), the faithful believer can now look forward to "eternal life" with Him. This is not the result of human works, since no one who has sinned against God can any longer be justified by these; it is God's grace which provides "sanctification." To be sanctified means to be set apart for God's use, to be made holy to Him. Those sanctified are called, appropriately, "saints" (as in 1 Cor. 1:2).

The only thing the sinner earns, ironically, is his own spiritual death (6:23). He does not earn salvation because this is a "gift," never a wage (recall 3:24). To receive "the free gift of God" is the finest outcome any human soul could ever hope to have: an eternity spent with a benevolent God.

Questions

1.) In the context of salvation, what is the relationship between law and grace—how can these two things work together without contradiction?

    a. Does grace nullify the need for law?

    b. Does obedience to law render useless the work of grace?

2.) In 6:2, Paul stated, "How shall we who died to sin still live in it?" What does it mean to "die to sin"? Does this mean that sin no longer *tempts* us? Does it mean that what tempted us prior to our baptism will tempt us no longer? Please explain.

3.) To present the members of your body as "instruments of righteousness to God," will there be certain recreational activities or lifestyles that you must avoid (6:12-13)? Will there be certain good habits that you must pursue? Or is Paul just talking figuratively here, and what you do in the body is of no consequence either way? Please explain.

4.) Why is being "enslaved to God" (6:22) a good thing, despite the negative connotation often associated with "slavery"? What does this enslavement necessarily imply?

Lesson Ten:
The Benefit of Freedom from Law's Condemnation (7:1-25)

Death Severs Earthly Allegiances (7:1-6): One's severance from his allegiance to sin—and his subsequent allegiance to Christ—is analogous to being legally unbound (freed; released) from a marriage. Paul speaks to those familiar with "the law" (7:1)—really, the law of *marriage*, which God implicitly ordained "from the beginning" (Mat. 19:4-6).

Marriage only has "jurisdiction" over those who are living; death effectively and permanently severs this union (7:2). However, if a man's wife leaves him (while he is still living) to become another man's wife, "she shall be called an adulteress"—one who has illegitimately violated her lawful marriage.[41] However, if her husband dies, she can legally become another man's wife since her first marriage no longer exists (7:3).

"Therefore" (7:4) implies a conclusion drawn from what was just said: death severs that which once bound one person to another. The institution of marriage does not die, but one can be dead to the institution (Mat. 22:30). Thus, "you [Christian] also were made to die" to the condemnation brought about by law (7:4). Once again, the condemnation of law did not die—it continues to condemn all other lawbreakers—but the believer died to its condemnation. The marriage illustration, then, is analogous but not perfect: in the illustration, the husband dies, liberating his wife from that which bound them together; here, it is (in effect) the *dead husband* who is liberated from his living wife. What is common between the two—and this is Paul's point—is that the death of one relationship makes possible the creation of a new relationship.

This "death" is real, but not literal: we do not literally die to become joined to Christ in a new union. But we *must* "die" to sever sin's mastery over us; our baptism symbolizes this death. (recall 6:3-7). Even so, someone did in fact die—one whose actual death validates our symbolic death: Christ (7:4). Through His death, we are freed from law's condemnation (since His death fulfilled the penalty of that condemnation), and thus we can be legally bound to Christ instead. We are not bound to a dead man, but to a Living Savior, "to Him who was raised from the dead."

One who has not died to the world (and to law's condemnation) can only bear "fruit for death"—i.e., the unproductive results of a godless life—and not "fruit" for God (7:5). However, once a person is joined to the Lord (1 Cor. 6:17), he can bear much "fruit" because of the Spirit of God who indwells him. The Spirit "gives life" to our souls and the good works we produce (John 6:63, 12:24, 15:1-6, and Gal. 5:22-23), as we will see in chapter 8. Likewise, the "newness of the Spirit"—the Spirit's regeneration of our souls (Titus 3:5)—contrasts with the "oldness of the letter" which offers no life but produces only death (7:6).

God's Law, Though It Condemns, Is Just (7:7-13): From what Paul has said, it might appear that the Law *itself* was the problem (7:7). Paul dismisses this in strong language: "May it never be!" God does not give defective or unjust laws; rather, His laws lead the human soul to life (Lev. 18:5, Luke 10:25-28). The purpose of God's codified laws was never to create problems but to magnify people's utter sinfulness and God's absolute holiness. The Law did not create the problem, but it could not solve it, either.

Paul draws upon his own experience as an example of what he means (7:7-13). Before understanding what coveting was, Paul considered himself "alive" (i.e., innocent). But when he learned the Law's teaching on coveting, it (the Law) revealed coveting within his own heart. Instead of standing favorably before God, he realized that he fell short of God's glory (recall 3:23); upon that realization, "sin became alive and I died" (7:9). "Died" here refers to the Law's condemnation of Paul as a *lawbreaker* rather than a law-*keeper*.

The commandment that exposed Paul's sin did not make the commandment itself sinful. The Law did not deceive Paul but enlightened him; sin is what deceived and "killed" him. "So then," regardless of who sins against it, God's law remains "holy and righteous and good" (7:12). The commandment of law declared sin to be "utterly sinful"—the cause of death to the human soul (7:13; see 1 Cor. 15:56).

The Struggle between One's Spirit and His Carnal Desires (7:14-25): This next section (7:14-25) explains why the Law (or simply, "law") is good and just, while the inclination of man's "flesh" is to pursue sin. This section is difficult for two reasons: first, the grammatical construction, though sound, is difficult to follow; second, there are disagreements over exactly what spiritual condition it is that Paul describes. Some believe he is describing himself (as a pious Jew) prior to becoming a Christian; others believe he describes his internal struggle *after* having become a Christian.

A godless heathen would never "joyfully concur[s] with the law of God" in his heart (7:22). And, while it is true that the struggle between good and evil does not evaporate once a person becomes a Christian (and may intensify), it is hard to reconcile phrases like "sold into bondage of sin" or "body of this death" with a Christian's state of being. But if one reads this section from the point-of-view of a pious Pharisee—as Paul most certainly had been—it should become clear that he speaks retrospectively, not presently. Granted, the present tense in which he narrates this ("I am …"; "I do …"; etc.) seems to undermine this at first. Yet we do the same thing when we narrate in the present tense that which had happened in the past: "Okay, so I am going out to my car, and I see this guy standing there, and he hands me this brochure, etc." Besides, Paul's intention here is to support the holiness of "the Law" (7:12–13)—in this case, the Law of Moses—and he wrote this section with that support in mind.

In this section (7:15–20), Paul is not speaking hypothetically but realistically and personally. While under the Law of Moses, he experienced an obvious struggle within himself: he knew what was good yet did not always do it; he also knew what was evil yet, because of the law of God in his heart, sought to avoid this.

Though he had been a God-fearing, law-abiding Pharisee, Paul could not be justified by appealing to his own good conduct, for he admits here that his conduct was not always good. Having given in to the temptation of sin even once, he was no longer able to justify himself, even though he continued to seek God's fellowship. Thus, he describes a war—really, a series of wars or a full-scale *battle*—between his God-seeking spirit and his carnal desires (Mat. 26:41).

If left to his own carnal nature, Paul's own sinful passions would have consumed him (7:17–20). The laws of God, however, provided a positive reinforcement of the good behavior with which he so passionately served the Lord (7:21–22). Thus, he rejoices over the benefits provided by these laws "in the inner man" (i.e., in his heart). Even so, the war continued to rage, and left him in a "wretched" state of being (7:23–24).

To recap (7:25): Paul admits that, as a pious Pharisee, he was a spiritual being who deeply desired fellowship with God and was devoted to His law. However, he was also a carnal man who continued to fall short of God's glory. Paul cannot mean here, "Who will set me free from having to obey God's laws?" for it is impossible to define faith apart from obedience. He also cannot mean, "Who will set me free from my physical sinful body?" or "Who will set me free from ever having to struggle against sin again?" for such statements are unsupported by the context and unrealistic. What Paul is saying here seems to be, in essence: "How can I, a man who struggles against sin yet longs to live in God's favor, be justified before Him?" The answer—and there is only one answer (John 14:6)—is Jesus Christ.

Questions

1.) According to 7:4–5, the purpose for being joined to Christ is to "bear fruit" for God.

   a. Can we bear this "fruit" if we are *not* joined to Christ (John 15:1–6)?

   b. What kind of "fruit" is God expecting from us (Gal. 5:22–23)?

   c. What does it mean to "bear fruit for death"?

2.) Some blame God's *law* for their problems, not sin: "I'm a good person; God has no right to be so critical of me." But is God's law at fault for calling attention to our sins (7:9–11)? Does the gospel cause us to sin, or do we sin against the gospel? In other words, where does the moral responsibility for sin belong?

3.) Even if Paul is describing himself (in 7:14–25) as a devout Pharisee, does his description also parallel the Christian's experience of trying to please God even while engaged in a battle against evil desires? If so, does this happen to every Christian, or only to those who have been excessively worldly prior to their conversion? Please explain.

Lesson Eleven:
The Benefit of the Spirit's Guidance
(8:1–17)

Freedom from Law's Condemnation (8:1–4): Paul states triumphantly, "There is now no condemnation for those who are in Christ Jesus" (8:1). "Now" is in sharp contrast with the implied "then" of his former experience as a pious Pharisee. "No condemnation" cannot mean that Christians are immune to sin or cannot fall from grace, since the Bible teaches otherwise (Gal. 5:1–4, Heb. 6:4–8, etc.). Rather, those "in Christ" are freed from the condemnation brought about by an unmerciful law of works.

The "law of…Christ" (8:2) refers not only to commandments but encompasses the entire prescription for salvation ("of life"). This law is also "of the Spirit" (from God), because the Spirit provides sanctification (1 Peter 1:3) and access to God (Eph. 2:18) through His ministerial work. The Spirit's work is carried out in the individual believer as well as the collective body (church) of the saints.[42]

In describing the Law as "weak" (8:3), Paul only refers to its limitations due to human inability to keep it perfectly. To overcome these limitations required a *divine Personage* (Christ) to do what no ordinary human could do. Through His obedience, Christ proved Himself worthy to provide a sin offering to God on our behalf (Heb. 10:5–10). "[I]n the likeness of sinful flesh"[43] refers to that which Christ represented, not something He became: though innocent of any crime (1 Peter 2:21), men condemned Him as a sinner (Mat. 26:65–66).[44]

In representing a sinner's death, Christ "condemned sin in the flesh" (8:3b): He proved that *every* sinner deserves to die. The "requirement" of God's law (8:4a) is death to the one who violates it. Yet, by sacrificing Himself *for* sinners, Christ robbed sin of its power *to* condemn them (see Heb. 2:14–15). While He fulfilled this requirement on the cross, we participate in this requirement symbolically through our baptism into His death (recall 6:3–7).

Two "Walks" Contrasted (8:5–17): In 8:4b, Paul contrasts those "who do not walk according to the flesh, but according to the Spirit." He takes the next several verses to expound upon this. To "walk" means to live in a certain way, with reference to one's regular habits. "Flesh" here refers to the satanic spirit of worldliness, sensuality, and pride which stand in defiance of God's will (Eph. 4:17–24, 1 John 2:15–17, etc.). To walk "according to the Spirit" means to live in fellowship with God. Notice the contrasts between the two "walks" (8:6–17):

One who walks according to the Spirit:	One who walks according to the "flesh":
Cannot walk according to the flesh	Cannot walk according to the Spirit
Sets his mind on things of the Spirit	Sets his mind on things of the flesh
Has life and peace in God (recall 5:1–2)	Is not at peace with God
Subjects himself to the will of God	Is in hostile opposition to God's will
Pleases God with his faithful obedience	Is unable to please God (Heb. 11:6)
Has the indwelling of the Spirit (1 John 4:13)	Does not belong to God and therefore does not have His Spirit indwelling him
His body is condemned to die, but his spirit is "alive because of righteousness"	His body *and* spirit are condemned
His body will be raised in glory by Christ "to a resurrection of life"	His body will be raised in shame "to a resurrection of judgment" (John 5:29)
Puts to death the deeds of the flesh	Indulges in deeds of the flesh (Gal. 5:19–21)
Is led by the Spirit of God	Is led by his self-serving lusts
Lives as a son (child) of God (Gal. 4:5–6)	Is enslaved by sin (John 8:34, Rom. 6:16)
As a legally adopted child of God, he has an inheritance from God (Eph. 1:9–11)	Since he has no relationship with God, is a stranger to Him without any inheritance
Will suffer in this life but glorified in the life to come (2 Cor. 4:16–18)	Will suffer in this life *and* in an eternal separation from God in the hereafter
Will live (John 6:40)	Will die (John 8:24)

To "set [one's] mind" on either the flesh or the Spirit means to fixate one's attention on that which he believes will bring him the greatest advantage (8:6–7). The pursuit of human cravings leads to (spiritual) "death"; to walk by the Spirit leads to (spiritual) life (Gal. 5:16). One experiences "life and peace" who walks by the Spirit (8:6). Yet, one who walks opposed to God's Spirit is "hostile" to God: he makes himself God's enemy and therefore has no life in him (James 4:4). Such a "mind" (heart) "cannot please

God" (8:8) because it operates in defiance of His will, His nature, and His commandments.

"However" (8:9) indicates a contrast, but only when certain conditions are met (as implied by the several "if" statements). Being "in the Spirit" is synonymous with walking "according to the Spirit" (recall 8:4). Only one who is filled with God's Spirit can walk with Him; he can only be filled with Him if he is "in Christ." It cannot be otherwise. The same Spirit is both "of God" and "of Christ," in that He is the dynamic agent in carrying out the divine work of the Godhead.[45] It is not necessary that we fully understand how the Spirit indwells us; it is only necessary to believe that He *does*, and that this indwelling produces necessary changes in the believer's life.

This change will not only be spiritual in nature, but bodily. The human body, still under the curse that God placed upon Adam (Gen. 3:17–19), is destined to die. It is in this sense that "the body is dead because of sin" (8:10). However, one's spirit can live to God even though his body will die. But God's power can also overcome physical death: as the Holy Spirit was involved in Christ's bodily resurrection from the dead, so He will be involved in our bodily resurrection (8:11).

Since the Spirit indwells the believer, "we are under obligation" to serve the One to whom we have given our allegiance (8:12; recall 6:12–18). Paul's "you must die" and "you will live" statements contrast God's condemnation and His justification through faith, not physical death versus physical life. While God's Spirit gives life to our souls, we must put to death the deeds of the body (8:13; see Gal. 5:19–21). Wicked habits, vices, addictions, and "every form of evil" (1 Thess. 5:22) must be identified, confronted, and removed. We cannot allow evil behavior to coexist with righteousness.

Those who are led by the Holy Spirit are called "sons of God" (8:14), which anticipates an inheritance with Him (Gal. 4:7).[46] Paul builds upon this relationship for a moment to drive home two points: first, its unnaturalness (since we are not natural sons); second, its supreme benefits (since we are now of God's family).[47] Jesus is the "only begotten [Son] from the Father" (John 1:14); those who enter into covenant with God are "adopted" sons (8:15). The transaction by which we were made "sons" is legal and binding, making us fully eligible for an inheritance.

The Spirit testifies *with* our spirit—not apart from or instead of it—that we are indeed "children of God" (8:16). The Spirit confirms that we have been obedient to the gospel commands by which we *become* "sons." These commands include but are not limited to baptism (see Gal. 3:26–27). Put another way: the Spirit is a legal witness to the reality and legitimacy of our sonship to God. *We* know what we have done, but (Paul says) so does God's *Spirit.* This is supremely important since our future inheritance—eternal life with God—depends upon the genuineness of our sonship (8:17).

Christ, as the only begotten of God, is the "heir of all things" (Heb. 1:2). However, He is willing to share this inheritance with those who believe in Him. In this way, we are "heirs *of* God and fellow heirs *with* Christ" (8:17, emphases mine). The promise of this inheritance remains conditioned upon our continued allegiance to Christ. A necessary part of this allegiance is our willingness to "suffer with Him," since we have been called for this very purpose (1 Peter 2:18–21). This suffering refers to whatever trials, losses, or persecutions we face specifically for the sake of Christ and His righteousness (Mat. 5:10–12). If one will not suffer for Christ, then neither will Christ glorify him.

Questions

1.) There is no condemnation for those who are "in Christ" (8:1). What does it mean to be "in Christ"? What does it *not* mean?

2.) Paul says that "those who are in the flesh cannot please God" (8:8). Given the context, what did he mean by this? What did he *not* mean?

3.) Paul says that we must "[put] to death the deeds of the body" (8:13). Is this necessary, or simply advisable? Is this something we do on our own or can we seek God's help in doing this?

4.) In 6:18, Paul referred to Christians as "slaves to righteousness"; in 8:14–16, he says we are "sons of God" and "children of God," and that we have "not received a spirit of slavery leading to fear again." So, which is it: are we "slaves" or are we "children"? Is it possible to be both at the same time? Please explain.

Lesson Twelve:

The Consolation of Hope and Divine Assurance (8:18–39)

Having just connected the Christian's suffering with future glorification (recall 8:17), Paul now takes a moment to expound upon this. In some ways, this exposition creates new questions even as it answers others. One thing is for certain: whatever losses we incur in this life for the sake of Christ will be more than compensated in the life to come (8:18).

Consequence of the Curse (8:19–22): The word "creation" (8:19) can also be "creature," depending on the context.[48] Here, "creation" seems the most natural conclusion. By the context and what we know elsewhere in Scripture, Paul's use of this word:[49]

- cannot refer to (good) angels, since they have—to our knowledge—never been "subjected to futility" (8:20).[50] "Futility" here means emptiness, vain things, fruitlessness, or whatever does not lead a person to God.[51]
- cannot refer to wicked demons or Satan, for they will never be freed from futility.
- cannot refer only to those who remain unbelievers, for the same reason as above.
- is not referring only to Christians since Paul mentions them later (8:23–25).

Thus, "creation" refers to the whole of physical nature in general (animals, birds, fish, plants, etc., and the entire inanimate physical world), which includes all men, regardless of their moral standing with God.

Paul's point: since all of creation was originally in subjection to Adam (Gen. 1:28–30), his sin affected everything under him. The entire creation, then, suffers under the curse for his moral disobedience. But there remains an "anxious longing" within creation for the restoration of that which was lost (8:19). This is not meant in a literal sense (as in a rehabilitated planet), but in the grand scheme of God's relationship with humankind. God did not create people (or their world) to suffer, but to live in fellowship with Him. Human suffering is the consequence of human sin; through Christ's redemption this suffering will not last forever. As a result, God's purpose for the "creation"—people and their world—will be fulfilled when the redeemed are brought into God's glory.[52]

This explanation seems unsatisfying to some, since it does not address how the physical creation will be "set free" if it will disappear (8:21). But Paul's language here is figurative—the personification of "the creation" indicates this—not literal; he speaks with a big-picture, end-of-all-things perspective, not about particular details. The physical world suffers for now but not forever; likewise, Christians suffer for now but not forever.

God's curse upon Adam's world was a direct response to Adam's sin (8:20). "Futility" implies hopelessness: without the redemption of human souls, all creation would be pointless. Yet "God's creation is not a grand failure"[53] since the salvation of the part (i.e., the redeemed) satisfies the purpose of the whole (i.e., the physical creation). Put another way: the redeemed could not have *become* "the redeemed" without the context of the entire creation. The "hope" of God's creation is entirely bound up in the redemption of God's people; apart from this salvation, all hope is gone.

Until the realization of this redemption, however, the physical world continues to suffer (8:21). The childbirth analogy (8:22) indicates that something good will come from suffering, even though the suffering itself may seem unbearable. Likewise, Christians also suffer (8:23)—and Paul did particularly (2 Cor. 11:23–28, etc.)—but good will come from this. The "we" reference here seems to refer to those who enjoyed the "first fruits of the Spirit" but includes all Christians, since all endure trials for their faith in Christ.

The Spirit's Intercession (8:23–27): The work of the Spirit within Christians is a pledge of good things to come: their "adoption as sons"; the "redemption of our body" (recall 8:11); and salvation itself (8:23–24). "In hope we have been saved," because our salvation is in the form of a promise, not yet fully realized or "seen." We have not yet seen God; we remain tethered to this life; we still live under the same curse that God imposed upon the entire world. Our hope is real but pertains to the invisible future, not the visible present (8:25; see 2 Cor. 4:16–18).[54]

The entire creation groans, the Christian groans, and "in the same way the Spirit … intercedes for us with groanings too deep for words" (8:26). "Weakness" (here) refers to our inability to express ourselves adequately to the Father, as regards what is best, what is right, and what agrees with His will; thus, the need for the Spirit's intercession. The Spirit does not groan as we do, as one subjected to the sufferings of this world, but pleads on our behalf.[55] The Spirit "helps our weaknesses"—"helps" comes from a Greek word used only here and in Luke 10:40, where Martha asked Jesus to tell Mary to give her a hand.[56]

Paul's expression, "the mind of the Spirit" (8:27), seems to be speaking of the actual mind of God's Spirit—an intelligent Personage of the Godhead distinct from but intimately united with the Father. In any case, God searches the mind of His Spirit, who Himself searches the minds (hearts) of His people. Thus, God the Spirit intercedes for the prayers of the saints, always according to the Father's will.

The Predestination of God's Church (8:28–30): Though the creation suffers, God will bring about good for His people (8:28). He has repeatedly proven in Scripture His ability to do this, even against impossible odds. "Those who love the Lord," "those who are called,"[57] and "those whom He foreknew" (8:29) all refer to the same people: Christ's spiritual church. The actions described in 8:29–30 apply to the entire body of Christ, not to any individual Christian:

- God **foreknew** the church: He knew prior to its establishment that it would be the only body of the redeemed ("there is one body"—Eph. 4:4).
- God **predestined** the church—the entire body of Christ, not each individual member—to conform to the image of His Son (Eph. 4:11–13). Before Christ's church ever came to be, God foreknew the nature and outcome of it.
- God, having foreknown and predestined this group of believers, then **called** that group out of the world (2 Cor. 6:16–18, 2 Thess. 2:13–14).
- God then **justified** all those who became part of this called-out group. In this case, it can be said that the entire group is "justified" since it is made up only of justified people.
- Being foreknown, predestined, called, and justified, the church is **glorified**. Notice this action is in the past tense. This speaks to reality

of the believer's justification and at the same time anticipates a glorious future (as in Eph. 2:6).

Our Victory through God's Justification (8:31–39): "What then shall we say to these things?" (8:31). God has not withheld anything from His church: if He has given us His Son, He will give us whatever else we need as well (8:32). Since God has justified us, no accusation or charge against Christians will have any legal or binding effect (8:33). Christ has died for us, but He now lives for us and serves as our Intercessor to the Father (8:34).[58] Faithful Christians have nothing short of the highest and most powerful authority *in the universe* supporting, protecting, and advocating for them.

If we are in fellowship with God, then no power can sever those who abide in His love from His salvation (8:35–39). Even so, this does not remove or make us immune to trials, heartache, persecution, or even martyrdom; Paul's citation (8:36) from Psalm 44:22 indicates that the Christian's suffering is not a new phenomenon. Nonetheless, not only are we victorious in Him in our world, but we shall celebrate Christ's victory throughout the eternity to come (8:37–39).[59]

Questions

1.) If, after a life of self-denial, battling against temptations, and disciplining yourself to walk with Christ, you stand favorably before God, will not your life on this earth be worthwhile?

   a. Can you see a link between this and how "the whole creation" will have served God's purpose through the redemption of His people?

   b. What if a Christian refuses to deny himself and endure hardships for Christ's sake? Will he be a partaker of the "glory that is to be revealed" (8:18)?

2.) "Hope" may be defined as a combination of desire and expectation (8:24–25). One cannot "hope" for something he does not desire or has no right to expect.

   a. Can a person who does not earnestly desire God hope to be in heaven? What does it mean to desire God?

   b. If a person claims to desire God but fails to obey Him, can he hope to be in heaven? If so, what would his hopeful expectation be based upon?

   c. If one does desire God above all other desires and lives in obedient faith to Him, should he doubt his future in heaven (see 1 John 2:28 and 3:19–22)?

3.) "God causes all things to work together for good to those who love God" (8:28). Why are *you* (or anyone else) unable to cause all things to work together for *your* good, both in this life and the life to come? (There are several answers.)

4.) Paul lists all sorts of external factors that cannot separate us from the love of God in Christ (8:35–39). Yet, we know that impenitence *can* separate us from His fellowship (Isa. 59:1–2, Gal. 5:4, 1 John 1:5–10, etc.). If one is separated from God's fellowship because of sin, then will be saved by His love, regardless?

Section Three:
The Righteousness of God (9:1—11:36)

Having laid out the doctrine of justification, Paul now turns to a different but related subject: the nation of Israel itself. The purpose for this is two-fold. **First,** to show that God was not negligent about promises He had made long ago to Israel. Rather than the gospel being an abandonment of those promises, Paul argues that the gospel of Christ expresses the "righteousness of God" to Israel. **Second,** even though Jews and Gentiles are equal in Christ, the Gentiles owed a tremendous debt of gratitude to the faithful remnant of Jews who had kept the promises of God alive until the gospel's unveiling. Paul wanted to set the record straight regarding what had transpired between God and Israel, and where everyone stands who is presently in Christ.

Lesson Thirteen:
God Has Not Failed in His Promises to Israel (9:1–33)

Paul begins this discussion by first expressing his great sorrow for—and great disappointment in—the Jewish nation. Only a relatively small number of Jews had come to Christ, even though they were the first to be invited (9:1–5).[60] Paul's disappointment is understandable; yet his compassion, while admirable, is difficult to comprehend, given how often the Jews had maligned, harassed, and even tried to kill him. Nonetheless, Paul cares deeply for his countrymen, and yet is about to say some things that the Jewish mind will find very difficult to hear—and he wants *them* to know that *he* knows this.

The Great Privilege Given to Israel (9:3–5): In a shocking admission, Paul states that he would rather be accursed if such a sacrifice could secure the salvation of his countrymen (9:3). This does not mean that he would gladly lose his *soul*—and willingly become God's enemy—if it meant the salvation of the Israelite nation, but it does mean that he would gladly give up his *life* for them.

Next, Paul expresses his respect for the Jewish nation and its benefits (9:4–5). The Israelites were more blessed, privileged, and honored by God than any nation on earth. Their Law (of Moses) was the greatest and most ethical legal document of the ancient world. God permitted them alone to build a tabernacle (and later, a permanent temple) for Him. They also had the writings of holy prophets to guide them—writings that embedded within them the promises of a coming Redeemer (Messiah). This Messiah came from their own people, and because of Him (and them) all the families of the earth have been blessed (Acts 3:24–26).

God's Choice of Israel (9:6–18): Despite God having offered salvation to the Gentiles did not mean He failed to keep His promises to the Jews. The spiritual people of "Israel" (i.e., Christians) now include those who are not Israelites by blood but are those justified by faith (Gal. 3:7–9, 6:15–16). Furthermore, Israel did not choose God, but God chose Israel (9:6–13). To highlight God's choice, Paul cites the case of Esau and Jacob: both were born to Isaac, but God directed the promise to continue through the lineage of Jacob rather than Esau. God made this designation even before the children were born, so as not to leave the decision to mere men (Gen. 25:23), and to show that it was not based upon either man's successes or failures.

"Jacob I loved, but Esau I hated" (9:13, cited from Mal. 1:2) does not mean that Esau was predestined to fail against his own will.[61] It certainly does not have anything to do with the final disposition of Esau's soul: all of Paul's references to Esau *and* Jacob have to do with their earthly circumstances, not their eternal destinations. Rather, Paul says that Esau's self-determined character consistently went against God's divine nature (Gen. 26:34–35, Heb. 12:15–17), and God knew ahead of time that this would be the case. Because of this, He prevented Esau from receiving the first-born inheritance from Isaac.

Paul's point here (9:14–15) is rhetoric: Did God wrong Esau in choosing Jacob over him? Or did God wrong the nation of Israel in choosing them over all other nations (see Deut. 7:7–8)? Israel had no problem in being God's select people; but just as God's sovereign will selected them (and not others), so He can select others (as well as them). This does not nullify the promises made to Israel, but simply makes promises to others as well. God did not need to seek Israel's permission or approval in showing mercy to those who are not Israelites. "There is no injustice with God"—i.e., He is just in all His dealings.

Upon first reading of 9:17, it may appear that God hardens a person's heart independent of his will. Yet Pharaoh—the ruler of Egypt during the time of Israel's exodus (Exod. 5:1ff)—made his own heart hard (or unyielding, resisting; see Heb. 3:7–19) to God *and* Moses. God never hardens anyone's heart that has not already chosen to stubbornly resist His will and refuse the truth. We have previously seen how God "gave over" to depraved minds those who had already abandoned Him and refused to honor Him as God (recall 1:21–27). Likewise, God's "hardening" of one's heart is not something He imposes upon a person but is a consequence of that person's own decisions. The phrase "whom He desires" (9:18) refers, then, to God's divine intervention in the matter: God did not have to show such mercy to Israel, nor did He have to push Pharaoh to the limit that He did. He intervened in both instances for the purpose of furthering His will, which was to bring salvation to all humankind.

Israel's Resistance of God's Will (9:19–33): Paul then anticipates the reply of an obstinate Jew: "Yes, but why does God still find fault in me, since I cannot resist the will of a sovereign God?" (paraphrase of 9:19). The implication is: If Israel had remained faithful, God never would have needed to usher in a redeeming Messiah—and the rest of humanity would have suffered as a result! If the Jews had not crucified Jesus, then the world would never have benefited from His sacrificial death! So how can God find fault with those who, despite their own errors, are carrying out His divine will?

Such talk is contemptuous since it portrays God's holy will as though it were in league with human rebellion. For this reason, Paul responds forcefully: "On the contrary, who are you, O man, who answers back to God [or, who calls God's judgment into question]?" (9:20) God does not make people guilty, nor does He punish the innocent; He does not force a person to be saved or condemned. But He *does* exercise sovereign will upon whomever He chooses.

For this reason, He capitalized upon Abraham's already good heart, but hardened Pharaoh's already wicked heart. Likewise, He promised destruction upon the wicked among Israel, but protected Israel's faithful remnant—thereby causing "all things to work together for good [for] those who love God" (Rom. 8:28). Israel had no basis by which to accuse God, just as the clay has no right to judge the potter (9:21). Just because God showed kindness to Israel did not mean He had no concern for non-Israelites who were facing "destruction" because of their sinful behavior (9:22).

The OT prophecies foretold of God's offer of salvation to Gentiles (9:25–26; see Isa. 49:5–6, where "nations" are Gentiles). The Jews should have been anticipating this, not scorning it, or standing in the way of it. The quotes from Hosea 1:10 and 2:23 initially applied to the estranged nation of Israel, but—like the dual-fulfillment of many OT prophecies—extended to the Gentiles as well. God was not only concerned for Israel, but He wanted *all* people to have fellowship with Him. In quoting from Isa. 10:22–23, Paul makes the point that, despite Israel having a covenant relationship with God (when the Gentiles did not), only a "remnant" (a small proportion) of Israel was actually "saved" (9:27–28).

While Israel had every advantage (recall 9:4–5), this did not guarantee their collective success. The prophets' writings are filled with numerous instances of their rebellion against God. And, if not for God's merciful intervention, Israel would have been obliterated like Sodom and Gomorrah (9:29, citing Isa. 1:9). Thus, Paul counters the Jews' argument by saying, in essence, "Here you [Jews] are upset that God has shown kindness to Gentiles, yet look how poorly your own nation has responded to the kindness He has shown to you! This not only undermines the strength of your argument but defeats it altogether."

Finally, Paul draws some powerful conclusions (9:30–32). Gentiles who lived faithfully to God were able to obtain righteousness even though they did not have the Law of Moses; the Jews did have the Law, but vainly tried to obtain righteousness through commandment-keeping rather than by faith. God accepts the humble faith of the Gentile but rejects the proud self-righteousness of the circumcised Jew (recall 2:25–29).

The Law was meant to lead Israel to Christ, and yet while the Jews had Christ in their very midst, performing numerous and unprecedented miracles, they rejected Him as their Messiah (9:33). Instead of embracing God's Son as their Redeemer, they hardened their heart against Him, just as they had long hardened their heart against God (Acts 7:51–53). Thus, the One who was the cornerstone of God's spiritual temple became to many of the Jews a "stumbling block"—something they tripped over because of their blindness (John 9:39–41) and obstinacy (1 Peter 2:7–8). Yet, to others, this same "stone" became the source of salvation.

Questions

1.) An overarching biblical principle is this: with great privilege comes great responsibility (Luke 12:47–48). How did this principle apply to the Jews? How does this principle also apply to Christians, in comparison to those who remain outside of Christ?

2.) God foreknew the selection of (the lineage of) Jacob over Esau before the two men were even born (9:6–13). God also foreknew what the Jews would do to Jesus (Acts 2:22–23), just as Jesus foreknew what Judas would do to Him (John 13:18–19). Does God's *foreknowledge* of an event or situation equate to Him *forcing* a predetermined outcome that violates the free will of every person involved? Please explain.

3.) Many Jews in Paul's day struggled with the fact that the gospel made both Jew and Gentile as equals. Instead of being thankful for what they had in Christ, some Jews were unhappy with who else was blessed.

   a. Might this same attitude prevail even among Christians today, especially toward those who were once particularly sinful and yet have come to Christ (Luke 15:11–32)? Or toward those who came to Christ late in life, while others have borne this responsibility for considerably longer (see Mat. 20:1–16)?

   b. Instead of resentment, what should Christians show such people—and why?

4.) Why was it important that God kept all His promises to the Israelites? (There are several answers.) What if He had failed to keep any promises to them—how would this affect His promises to *us*?

Lesson Fourteen:
God's Righteousness Shown to Israel
(10:1–21)

The Jews Sought Justification through Law (10:1–4): Once again, Paul expresses his earnest desire for the salvation of his countrymen, but he also realizes that this will never happen unless they come to Christ. No one could fault the Jews for lacking in religious passion and enthusiasm; yet passion is no replacement for righteousness (10:1–4). Zeal without knowledge leads to erroneous conclusions, not righteous obedience (see John 16:1–3). "Knowledge" here refers specifically to what has God revealed through His law, prophets, and apostles.

As a rule, the Jews sought justification through law-keeping rather than submission to "the righteousness of God" (10:3). Christ is the fulfillment (or aim; goal; completion) of all that the Law of Moses foreshadowed, yet the Jews rejected Him. Thus, the unconverted Jews tried to maintain two incompatible positions: they claimed allegiance to God's Law even while they denied the objective of that Law (see John 5:39–40, 45–47).

Belief in and Confession of Christ (10:5–13): The Jews virtually idolized Moses (John 9:28–29) yet did not fully listen to him. Moses had already stated what Paul has just declared (10:5): to be justified by law, one must keep it perfectly (see Gal. 5:3 and James 2:10). Yet such justification is impossible, since all people fail to be law-keepers (recall 3:23). Because of this, God has provided through Christ a means for all people to be justified by faith, not law. One does not have to wonder how he will "ascend" or "descend" where it is humanly impossible to go for this justification; he only needs to believe in the One who *has* gone there.[62] "[I]n your heart" (10:6) means "through faith": just as Israel was to demonstrate faith in God to find favor with Him, so one must now demonstrate faith in the Son of God for the same reason.

"Confessing" and "believing" (10:8–10) are works of human faith. Salvation is *not* a work of human faith, yet it is impossible *without* this faith, and "faith without works is dead" (James 2:26). In faith, one must confess that "Jesus is Lord"—in other words, that God did indeed send Him down from heaven (John 6:32–33, 1 John 2:22–23). Likewise, he must believe that God did indeed raise Jesus from the grave, for without this there is no hope for overcoming the curse of sin (recall 8:20–22; see 1 Cor. 15:13–19). By believing that God resurrected His Son, one also believes that God will raise *himself* from the death of his spiritual condemnation.

Paul is not saying, "Just say 'Jesus is Lord' and acknowledge His resurrection, and there is nothing else you must do to be saved." Instead, to "confess" means to speak and live in agreement with that confession; to "believe" means to do whatever else is necessary to support such convictions.[63] "Confessing" and "believing" are not the only actions required for salvation but are *at least* required. No one who confesses and believes in Christ will "be disappointed [or, put to shame; have cause for regret]" (10:11–13).[64] This is true because Christ has made salvation possible to all people; He has given sufficient proofs that He was sent from heaven and did resurrect from the dead; He promises salvation to every person who believes in and confesses Him. No one who does what He requires will seek Him in vain.

No Excuse for Failing to Believe in Christ (10:14–21): For one to hear this good news of God's salvation, someone must preach it (10:14–15). ("Preacher" here does not refer to a full-time position, as we are familiar with today, but simply means a herald or proclaimer, which could be any believer.) Paul here alludes to the OT prophets who were "sent," which means they did not speak on their own authority but heaven's. Having such a heavenly proclamation, they were worthy of commendation (Isa. 52:7). Thus, the Jewish prophets long anticipated the message of Christ's gospel. If anyone should have responded favorably to this gospel, it should have been the Jews.

Yet Israel also had a long history of choosing not to obey good news (10:16). The prophet Isaiah asked in exasperation of this failure to respond, "Lord, who has believed our report?" (Isa. 53:1). While the Jews could not confess or believe in Christ if they had never heard of Him, the "word of Christ" (10:17) was cause enough for them to put their faith in Him. Even so, Paul rhetorically poses the question, in essence: "Maybe they have never heard of Him?" Yet for centuries the Jews had heard the prophets' "voice" (10:18; quote is from Psalm 19:4).

Paul continues rhetorically: "Maybe the Jews just didn't understand?" Yet even as far back as Moses, God had been prophesying of a universal salvation (10:19; quote is from Deut. 32:21); and Isaiah prophesied that the Gentiles ("nation") would be recipients of this salvation (10:20; quote is from Isa. 65:1). Paul concludes his point (10:21): the problem was not that the Jews had not heard or could not understand the gospel of Christ; instead, it was that their hearts were "disobedient" and "obstinate" toward God's prophets to begin with (see Isa. 65:2, Jer. 6:16–19, Amos 4:6–12, and Acts 7:51–53). Thus, the Gentiles "found" God, even though they had long been ignorant of Him; in contrast, the Jews resisted the Son of God, even though they were blessed with divine oracles concerning Him (recall 3:1–2, 9:3–5).

Questions

1.) Having "zeal without knowledge" (10:2) is common in contemporary, mainstream Christianity. But is zeal itself something to avoid? Is it any better to have knowledge without zeal?

2.) What does Paul mean by "a righteousness based on faith" (10:6)? Does merely claiming to have faith make us righteous? Will *any* "faith" lead to righteousness with God?

3.) Paul declared that "whoever will call upon the name of the Lord will be saved" (10:13).

   a. What does it mean to "call upon the name of the Lord"?

   b. What does the Lord require of one who calls upon His name?

4.) Paul wrote, "So faith comes from hearing, and hearing by the word of Christ" (10:17). Yet, faith is not the automatic result of having heard the gospel (Heb. 4:2). Why is this? What does it mean to have "faith" in God as opposed to merely "hearing" His message?

Lesson Fifteen:
God's Righteousness Shown to Gentiles (11:1–36)

God's Gracious Choice of Israel (11:1–6): Even though the nation of Israel had long been "disobedient and obstinate"—and even though God punished them for this resistance—it is not accurate to say that God had rejected His people *because* He punished them. The fact that His Son was born an Israelite is proof of this. Paul made this even more personal: the fact that he himself (a Jew) was a citizen of the kingdom was also proof of this (11:1)—and no one was prouder of his ancestral heritage than Paul (Gal. 1:13–14). "God has not rejected His people" (11:2) does not mean that God justified all Jews simply because they were Jews. God justifies people by their faith, not their ethnicity (Heb. 11:6).

On the other hand, even during Israel's darkest hours, there had always remained a remnant of believers who held fast to God's promises and obeyed His commandments. This was God's message to the prophet Elijah, who thought he alone *was* the "remnant" (11:2–4; see 1 Kings 19:13–18). However, the fact that God entrusted the remnant with these promises was not Israel's choice, but God's (11:5–6). This grace—a gift of God—removed any basis for Israel's boasting, for God could have just as easily chosen any other nation for this same purpose. Thus, even the remnant's preservation was not dependent upon their "works" (of Law) but their faith in God.

God's Salvation Given to Gentiles (11:7–15): "What then?" Paul asks rhetorically (11:7). In other words, "What is the natural conclusion to the matter under discussion?" While many Israelites sought justification through zealous works, they did not obtain it. The "chosen"—so identified because of their *faith* in Him—*were* justified, but by faith and not law-keeping. Israelites who sought God through any means other than faith were "hardened," which means they closed their heart to God's kindness and the opportunity for divine salvation (recall 2:4). To underscore his point, Paul cites examples from the OT (11:8–10; quotes are from Isa. 6:9–10 and Psalm 69:22–23).

While not all of Israel "stumbled"—disbelieved because of their hardness of heart—the many who did stumble gave opportunity for God to show His kindness to others (11:11). Thus, "salvation has come to the Gentiles," which was God's eternal purpose all along. Ideally, having offered to the Gentiles that which was promised to Israel would "make jealous" those Israelites who still resisted Christ's gospel (recall 10:19–20). The intent was for them to draw near to God by faith; proportionately few, however, responded in this way (see Acts 13:44–49).

Paul then addresses the Gentile Christians directly (11:12–16). He wants them to know that he is not saying such things to alienate his countrymen, but to provoke them to seek God through faith. To bring Jews to the gospel through his ministry to the Gentiles would "magnify" Paul's ministry: it would make it even more worthwhile. If by having rejected their Messiah the Jews were instrumental in ushering in salvation to the world, then their acceptance of Christ would lead to "life from the dead"—a resurrection of the hope of Israel through the power of their Redeemer.

The Remnant Preserves the Whole (11:16–32): The "first piece of dough" and "root" illustrations (11:16) allude to the "first fruits" concept in the Law of Moses (Lev. 23:10, Num. 15:18–21; see 1 Cor. 15:20). If one dedicated a remnant of his crop to God, then God would bless his entire harvest. The lesser portion sanctified the greater; the parts sanctified the whole. The "root" is the faithful remnant of Israel who kept the promises of the Redeemer alive through their faith in God; the "branches" are those Jews and Gentiles who were recipients of these promises through their acceptance of the gospel.

Jews are "natural branches" which came naturally from the root of the olive tree. Gentiles are as "wild" (or foreign) branches which had to be "grafted" in (11:17–24). The "olive tree" itself is Christ, whose identity and mission as Messiah sprouted directly from the root of God's promises and prophecies to Israel. Paul thus warns the Gentiles not to forget that it was not them but the Jewish remnant who kept the promises of God alive by faith (11:18). They must not, therefore, hold Jews in contempt or think lightly of their role in the gospel of Christ. Gentiles did not support the root but were blessed because the root supported them.

Paul then anticipates a Gentile's smug response: "Branches were broken off so that I might be grafted in" (11:19). In other words, "Because not all Jews were faithful, we have a legitimate right to take their places." While

Paul agrees with this (11:20), he clarifies the situation. If Jews are justified by faith, then Gentiles are justified in the same way; however, if Jews are removed because of unbelief, then Gentiles will be removed for the same reason. God's kindness is conditional; if the conditions are no longer met, then His kindness will be replaced with divine wrath (11:21–22). Even so, there is still hope for those Jews who had not yet believed: if they do respond to God in faith, then they who were once "broken off" will also be "grafted in" (11:23–24).

In this last section of this chapter (11:25–36), Paul admits that a "mystery" has been revealed: the Gentiles are now included in God's covenant of salvation (see Eph. 3:1–11). This once-hidden message could not have been proclaimed except for a "partial hardening" of Israel (11:25). This "partial hardening" refers to the *unbelieving* part of Israel but not the *entire* nation of Israel. As it was, the remnant of faithful believers preserved the nation of Israel, to the extent that God's purpose could be carried out through them.[65] The "fullness of the Gentiles" seems to refer to an era (or period) rather a specific number of people being saved or lost. In this sense, it refers to the time in which believing Gentiles entered the kingdom of God while unbelieving "sons of the kingdom" (Jews) did not (see Mat. 8:11–12). This era would end upon the destruction of Jerusalem (AD 70), since after that time the Jewish nation lost all distinction as God's covenantal people.

"And so all Israel will be saved" (11:26) cannot mean that every single Israelite will be saved, since God will not save anyone who refuses to put his faith in Him. "All Israel" is in parallel to how the redemption of the "whole creation" through the salvation of its remnant (recall 8:18–22): the whole will be justified (made worthwhile) by the redemption of the part (recall 9:29).

Thus, the faithfulness of the remnant of Israel ushered in the Savior of the world, so that all who are saved—whether Jews or Gentiles—owe a debt of gratitude to these believers. The quote (in 11:26–27) is from Isa. 59:20–21 and anticipates a time during the reign of Messiah when the shame of Israel's sins and captivities will be removed upon the establishment of a new covenant (see Jer. 31:31–34 and Heb. 8:8–13). The gospel of God outlines this new covenant, which Christ brought to life with His own blood (Mat. 26:26–29). Those who enter this covenant become members of Christ's church.

While the unconverted Jew is an "enemy" to the believing (Gentile), this does not mean God has no concern for him—or for all unbelieving Israelites (11:28). God's gifts, kindness, etc. toward the Israelites have not been given in vain (11:29). Just as He mercifully gave salvation to the Gentiles, though they were once disobedient to Him, God can just as easily do the same for disobedient Jews (11:30–31). In so doing, God has "shut up [or, silenced] all in disobedience" (11:32): no one can justify himself based on works since *all* (Jews and Gentiles) have disobeyed God's laws (Gal. 3:22). Yet now every sinner can receive mercy and forgiveness through a system of justification by faith.

God's Righteousness Extolled (11:33–36): These final verses appropriately express Paul's personal appreciation for the work of God toward the salvation of men (quotes are from Isa. 40:13–14). Whatever God has done has been for our human benefit and to the praise of His own glory. This hymn of praise (a.k.a. doxology) also serves as a fitting conclusion to the doctrinal section of *Romans* (chapters 1—11), wherein "the righteousness of God" is revealed through the gospel and every person is justified by his faith in this righteousness: "Amen."

Questions

1.) Some Christians today exhibit the so-called "Elijah syndrome" (11:2–4) in thinking they are the only ones left who are faithful, and everyone else has abandoned God (or is not as sincere as *they* are). Why is this unfounded? How can this mentality be avoided?

2.) While we may talk openly about divine grace, some Christians still tend to put more stock in what *they* do than in what *God* does (11:6). Why is this? (There may be several answers.)

3.) Paul goes to great lengths in this chapter to highlight the faithful remnant of Israel. Do you suppose that Christ's church—the worldwide brotherhood of those baptized into Him—also has a faithful remnant, or will Christ save anyone who simply identifies as a Christian?

4.) Notice that "kindness" (salvation) and "severity" (judgment) both come from the same God (11:22). What deciding factor(s) determines whether He will show one or the other? Are Christians exempt from experiencing His severity?

SECTION FOUR:
THE RIGHTEOUSNESS OF GOD PRODUCES A RIGHTEOUS LIFE
(12:1—15:33)

HAVING SUCCESSFULLY ARGUED THE CONCEPT OF "JUSTIFICATION BY FAITH," Paul now proceeds to the practical application of his letter to the Roman Christians. The heart and conduct of one justified by faith must agree with the God in whom he has *put* his faith. Having entered a covenant relationship with God, he must now continue to abide by its terms. This is as true today as it was when Paul penned these words (12:1—15:33).

Lesson Sixteen:
Righteous Conduct toward Fellow Christians
(12:1–21)

The Believer's Transformation by Grace (12:1–2): One's "newness of life" (recall 6:4) must affect every aspect of his life in a full surrender to Christ (12:1–2). "Presenting" oneself to God calls to mind the sacrificial system of the Law of Moses. But the Christian's offering is not a dead sacrifice, like the sheep and bulls offered on the ancient altar. Rather, he is a "living and holy sacrifice," implying a functional life worship. "Spiritual service" can be rendered "rational, sacred service"[66]: it is spiritual because of its type; it is intelligent (or rational; logical) because of those who offer it.

"Conform" means to imitate the likeness of something; "transform" means to be *changed* from one form to another. Being "conformed to this world" means to identify with it; genuine transformation, however, requires a complete renewing of one's mind (Eph. 4:22–24). One whose heart is "conformed to this world" cannot properly offer gifts and sacrifices to God, being hostile to Him (recall 8:6–9). Those justified by faith must change (i.e., be transformed); this change will be visible, radical, and life-altering;

"The renewed mind induces a new life."[67] God alone is qualified to define what is "good and acceptable" service (Heb. 12:28–29).

Every Part Contributes to the Whole (12:3–8): This next section (12:3–8) is like what Paul has said elsewhere (1 Cor. 12:12–28). Even though each Christian fulfills a priestly action in his service to God (1 Peter 2:9), no Christian is to think himself "more highly" than any other. Humility is the grease that keeps the machinery of Christian service effective and efficient (Mat. 18:1–4). The opposite of humility is pride, which only produces friction, tension, and unnecessary breakdowns in fellowship.

The analogy between the church and a human body (12:4–5) is an excellent one. The body is a working unit, comprised of smaller parts, organs, and systems. No part works alone, even though some do have a greater responsibility than others (e.g., the heart versus a finger). All its parts are meant to work in concert, not separately. So it is with the church: the "many members" have different functions, responsibilities, and measures of faith, but no one person acts alone or calls himself "the church" (or even "a" church). Christ's body is not divisible; despite any apparent dissimilarities, we "are all one in Christ Jesus" (Gal. 3:29). Therefore, each person's gifts, service, talents, exhortation, etc., must not be compared to another's, for this serves no good purpose. Christians are never in competition with each other.

God gives these "gifts"—whether miraculous (as was sometimes the case in Paul's day) or not (as in our present case)—to Christians according to God's grace (12:6a). God only gives gifts for good reason; thus, it is the Christian's responsibility to discover the purpose of his gifts and to exercise them according to that purpose (12:6b–8). One who prophesies, serves, teaches, exhorts, etc., is to do so to the best of his ability—which may be different than someone else who exercises the same gift.

What God Expects Christians to Do (12:9–21): Having instructed us to exercise our individual gifts, Paul follows with a list of general acts of service. These virtues and behaviors form a composite picture of what every Christian ought to "look" like:

- ❏ **"Let love be without hypocrisy"** (12:9)[68]: Love is to be "unfeigned" (1 Peter 1:22–23) and visibly demonstrated (1 John 3:18). Fake love or love without action is useless to the one who claims it, the one to whom it is directed, and the One in whose honor it is offered.

- ☐ **"Abhor what is evil; cling to what is good"** (12:9): A Christian cannot merely dislike sin but must hate it; it must repulse him. Likewise, he cannot passively agree with what is good, but must tenaciously pursue and lay hold of it (1 Thess. 5:21–22).
- ☐ **"Be devoted to one another in brotherly love"** (12:10): A Christian is to honor the family relationship we all enjoy in Christ (2 Peter 1:7). He must not merely acknowledge its existence but devote himself to its growth, success, and propagation.
- ☐ **"Give preference to one another in honor"** (12:10): Paradoxically, true greatness (in God's sight) comes through humility, which requires a preferment of others over oneself (Mat. 20:26–28, Phil. 2:3–4). This also implies giving others mercy and the benefit of doubt as opposed to rushing to judgment (Mat. 7:1–2, James 4:11–12).
- ☐ **"not lagging behind in diligence, fervent in spirit, serving the Lord"** (12:11): Service rendered to the Lord must be offered with zeal, enthusiasm, and purposeful intention. Laziness and slothfulness are not hallmarks of godly virtue but imply disrespect and unbelief. Cold indifference ruins "gifts" offered to God (Mal. 1:6–14); instead, our service (like our love for one another—1 Peter 1:22) is to be "fervent [lit., boiling (hot)]" with zeal and earnestness.
- ☐ **"rejoicing in hope, persevering in tribulation"** (12:12): All Christians have need of endurance (Heb. 10:36), but without a sufficient hope, there is no incentive for this. A strong and realistic hope contributes to a strong and enduring faith (2 Tim. 1:12).
- ☐ **"devoted to prayer"** (12:12): This does not refer to incidental prayers, but one's commitment to prayer as a lifestyle (Eph. 6:18, Col. 4:2). Prayer is our lifeline from earth to heaven; without it, we cannot access any spiritual blessings "in Christ" (Eph. 1:3) or petition God on behalf of others.
- ☐ **"contributing to the needs of the saints, practicing hospitality"** (12:13): "Hospitality" comes from a Greek root word which means "fond of guests" or "lover of strangers."[69] This refers to Christian "strangers" (3 John 1:5–8) or "prisoners" (Heb. 13:1–3). Paul's point is that Christians are to take care of one another.
- ☐ **"Bless those who persecute you…"** (12:14): This does not mean, "Be indifferent toward the harm inflicted upon you," or, "Pretend it doesn't hurt." It means, "Do your part to absorb the loss or harm inflicted upon

you so that God may be glorified in your choosing to do what is right despite the consequences" (see Mat. 5:44–47).

- ❑ **"Rejoice…, weep…"** (12:15): Just as our possessions are common between us (as needed), so our hearts are to be as one heart (1 Cor. 12:26, James 5:13–20). We should never be so self-absorbed that we think only of our own welfare and neglect the needs and concerns of others. Likewise, we are not to begrudge another's prosperity ("If only that had happened to me!") or gloat over his misfortune ("It's a good thing that didn't happen to me!").
- ❑ **"Be of the same mind…"** (12:16): "Same mind" does not mean "same opinion," unanimous consensus, or groupthink. The context has to do with a shared resolve to honor Christ's doctrine. No group of Christians will ever be of the exact same opinions; however, every church that invokes Christ's name must conform to and habitually practice His teaching (1 John 2:4–6, in principle).
- ❑ **"Never pay back evil for evil … be at peace with all men …"** (12:17–20): It is natural for the worldly individual to seek vengeance and retaliation for crimes committed against him. Yet Jesus set a different example for us (1 Peter 2:23). Christians are to be peacemakers (Mat. 5:9) and pursuers of peace (Heb. 12:14), "so far as it depends upon you." "Coals" are not meant to inflict injury or punishment but force a change of the perpetrator's heart by shaming him with kindness and good deeds (Prov. 25:21–22).
- ❑ **"Do not be overcome by evil, but overcome evil with good"** (12:21): Or "Stop being conquered by the evil (thing or man)," but "drown the evil in the good."[70] A Christian may not overcome another person's evil directed against him, but he can overcome evil in himself.

Elders should direct to this passage every Christian who comes to them and asks, "What should I be doing?" or "What can I do to help this congregation?" Nearly every Christian can do nearly every one of these actions. Furthermore, these are all *basic expectations*: they are the *least* that should be done.

Questions

1.) What does it mean to be "conformed to this world" (12:2)?

   a. What is the purpose of being transformed and renewed in one's mind?

   b. Can a person offer acceptable service to God if he resists this instruction?

2.) Compare the attitudes and behaviors in 12:9–21 with:
   - The criteria Jesus will use to judge His people (Mat. 25:31–46).
   - The definition and activity of love (1 Cor 13:4–7).
   - The developmental growth and exercise of faith (2 Peter 1:5–7).

   What consistent patterns do you see regarding what Christ expects of those who identify with Him? How will this benefit all those who conform to these?

3.) When Paul spoke of vengeance (12:17–21), he only dealt with conduct for which we are responsible, not wrongful conduct done against us. How is it possible to be controlled by another person's evil? (There are several possible answers.)

Lesson Seventeen: Righteous Conduct toward Secular Government (13:1–14)

Christians and Secular Authority (13:1–5): The proper response to governmental authority might have been a difficult subject for Christians living in the capital of a pagan, ungodly empire. This remains a difficult subject even today, although some Christians deal with it more emotionally than realistically. In an extreme view assumes that allegiance to Christ nullifies any allegiance to his government. The other extremity assumes that Christians are to obey whatever the government says in order not to violate passages like this one (13:1–5).

While God does not prevent governments from being wicked or unjust—even toward Christians—He is concerned with how His saints conduct themselves toward them. This is the main reason for Paul's instructions here. Some related passages include:

- **Acts 5:29:** "We must obey God rather than men"—Christians cannot obey laws of the land that violate our preeminent allegiance to God. On the other hand, this passage does not teach that we cannot follow *any* civil laws made by ungodly men.
- **1 Tim. 2:1–2:** Christians are to pray for those in authority, for their rulers' sakes as well as their own. Notice that the moral disposition of the "kings" is irrelevant.
- **Titus 3:1:** Christians are "to be subject to rulers, to authorities, to be obedient [to their laws], to be ready for every good deed" (bracketed words added). The issue here is our respect for God's authority, not necessarily whether we agree with the laws of the land.
- **1 Peter 2:13–17:** Christians are to honor those who have governing authority over their land, wherever they live. By obeying the laws of the land, those who might charge Christians of being lawbreakers, traitors, or anarchists would have no valid accusation.

Paul's (and Peter's) instructions on one's attitude toward government are not meant to be comprehensive but are general and apply to normal circumstances. Unusual, extraordinary, and even unprecedented circumstances require more specific direction than what we have been given, even though Paul's words here still provide a foundation for *all* such discussions.

Man-made laws are, in the most basic sense, meant to govern society, protect the rights and lives of law-abiding citizens, and punish criminals. Such laws are *not* meant to define, or interfere with, what Christians are called to do; even Jesus spoke of the separation of church and state (Mat. 22:17–22). The idea of seeking "permission" from governing authorities to carry out our God-given responsibilities as Christians manifests a great misunderstanding of this passage. On the other hand, becoming a Christian does not free a person from all the constraints of and obligations to civil law. Since God has given permission for secular authorities to exist, to purposely (or carelessly) disobey them defies God's own ordinance (law).

However, just because God allows a government to exist does not mean He sanctions its every decision or legislation. The Roman Empire was anything but godly; the same might be said for our American government. "God may and does tolerate governments in doing wrong, just as he does men in sinning, but he sanctions neither the wrong nor the sin."[71] To "submit" to such a government does not mean we do so blindly or without understanding; rather, it means we put ourselves under the control of this government voluntarily and for the right motives—above all, to honor God and set a good example for men.

Disobedience to human laws not only brings punishment from the government itself, but also a condemnation from God.[72] Unnecessary violation of civil law would then be against our conscience as well as against the governing authority. In this passage (13:3–4), Paul supports capital punishment (i.e., execution by the sword) and expects governments to exercise this right as a "minister of God" toward those who deserve it (see Acts 25:11).

Rendering All that Is Due (13:6–10): No Christian likes to pay taxes, especially to a secular government, but this does not (in itself) violate one's allegiance to Christ (13:6–7). In paying taxes, Christians are honoring God's authority, not giving an endorsement to all that government does with its money. For example, Jesus supported paying the Jewish the temple tax (Mat. 17:24–27), even though this indirectly supported those who would later conspire against His life (John 11:49–53). Jesus also supported paying taxes to Rome—the very government which would later authorize His own execution. "Render to all what is due them"—the one to whom the debt is owed is not the point here; rather, it is that God's people are not to be remiss in paying their debts (Mat. 22:15–22). Debts are like promises; refusing to pay them is equivalent to breaking a promise. Just as God is faithful to fulfill all His promises to men, so Christians must be faithful to fulfill theirs.

The deepest "debt" any of us has toward one another is not in the form of taxation, but love (13:8–10). Paul uses "debt" here figuratively, as a sort of play on words from the previous discussion on taxation. Love is, in essence, a "debt" that will never be paid up, a duty that is never complete. As God's love for us is continual and unconditional, so should ours be toward others, and especially toward the brethren (1 John 4:7–21). Love is the foundation of all moral laws (Gal. 5:14), since all other laws of God rest upon and find their completion in love. The demonstration of love is itself the "royal law" (James 2:8) since it reflects the King's own nature (1 John 4:8). One who shows love to his neighbor will always do him good and not harm, regardless of what action is taken (Mat. 7:12, Luke 10:29–37).

Now Is the Time to Act (13:11–14): Seeing that we have a finite existence on this earth, we have little time to carry out all our Christian duties and obligation. This ought to create a sense of urgency, not complacency or procrastination (13:11). To "awaken from sleep" is a mild rebuke; in other words, "If you have been lethargic in your moral responsibilities, it is time to wake up and be busy with them!" "Few Christians are ever as wide awake as they should be."[73]

While the world sinks into darkness and oblivion, Christians are to be a source of light and activity (Eph. 5:7–14). This means our behavior must match the seriousness of our ministry. "The night is almost gone"—in this context (13:12), "night" refers to this earthly life; "day" refers to an endless life with God. One must "lay aside" the "deeds of darkness"—i.e., the attitudes and behaviors that are associated with the corrupted earthly life (recall 8:12–13). In place of these things, he must "put on" that which God gives him: the "armor of light." "Let us behave properly as in the day" (13:13)—i.e., let us live as though we are already in the eternal "day" of fellowship with God. The following behaviors have no place in that fellowship:

- ❏ **Carousing and drunkenness:** "Carousing" comes from a Greek word which implies revelry, rioting, and a "letting loose" of one's inhibitions.[74]
- ❏ **Sexual promiscuity and sensuality:** "Sexual promiscuity" refers to lying down on a couch or bed—here, for the purpose of sexual intercourse.[75] "Sensuality" refers to unrestrained lust, filthy-mindedness, or any kind of sexual indulgence (Eph. 4:19).
- ❏ **Strife and jealousy:** These refer to quarreling, bickering, and contention. These behaviors also include the worldly attitudes that spawn them, as in coveting what someone else has or being unhappy that they have it (James 3:13–18).

"But put on the Lord Jesus Christ"—lit., clothe yourself with Christ (Gal. 3:27). In ancient times, a king would put royal raiment (garments) upon a person whom that king wanted to honor and have identified with him (see Esther 6:7–8, Zech. 3:3–5, Luke 15:22, etc.). Such honor and identification, of course, required that person to be responsible and rightly represent the one whose clothes he wore (Mat. 22:8–12). We do not put on a garment merely *belonging* to Christ, but we put on *Christ*. He does not force us to put Him on but only provides the opportunity. Whether or not we put Him on is up to each one of us.

Questions

1.) Paul wrote, "There is no authority except from [or by] God, and those which exist are established by God" (13:1). What does this mean? What does it *not* mean?

2.) There is no question that secular taxes are subject to misuse, wasteful spending, and other forms of corruption and mismanagement. Thus, a Christian might argue that any money that goes to the government in the form of taxes could go instead toward the work of God's kingdom (evangelism, benevolence, missionary work, etc.).

   a. Is this argument valid?

   b. Does this argument, even if it is valid, nullify one's responsibility to pay taxes?

3.) Why do we "owe" love to one another—what caused this "debt" (13:8)? Does this reduce our every act of love to a kind of "payment"? Please explain.

4.) What does it mean to "put on" Christ (13:14)? Does this mean "be baptized," or (because Paul was talking to Christians) something more than this?

Lesson Eighteen: Righteous Conduct of the Strong and Weak (14:1—15:13)

Paul now turns his attention to another aspect of Christian duty: dealing with those who are "weak in faith." While primary responsibility lies with the "strong," since these know better and are expected to exercise a more mature disposition, both parties are to accept one another in a mutually beneficial arrangement (15:7; see 1 Cor. 10:14–33 and Col. 2:16–23).

Differences of Conscience (14:1–12): To "accept" a fellow believer (14:1) means to receive him into fellowship, to treat him like family. "Weak" here does not mean incompetent or unwilling, but unable, due to the (yet) lack of mature faith, knowledge, or experience. The strong brother is not to accept a weaker brother only to criticize his motives and actions, but as a fellow and equal brother in Christ (Eph. 3:6, Gal. 3:28).

To illustrate this, Paul uses examples of eating meats versus vegetables, or the honoring of one day (i.e., a religious holy day) versus regarding all days equally. While we can still use these same examples, the principle employed here goes far beyond them. Each believer belongs to God, not to another believer (1 Cor. 6:19–20); each Christian is a servant of Christ and is thus not a slave to another brother's preference or opinion (1 Cor. 7:23, Gal. 5:1). It is unjust for one brother to "judge" [lit., sharply criticize or condemn] his brother based on private convictions. It is the Lord who makes us stand (14:4), not one another; to "stand" means to be justified (recall 5:1–2). If God justifies a person, it is irrelevant who else does or does not justify him (recall 8:33).

"Each person must be convinced in his own mind" (14:5)—that is, concerning opinions. The context here does not concern different interpretations of doctrine but matters not specifically defined by doctrine. You have your private convictions and I have mine; however, I cannot force my personal convictions upon you, nor can you judge me because I do not share yours. The word of God should already condition such convictions— i.e., *no* conviction is justifiable which violates the attitude or behavior of

Christ (Phil. 2:5, 1 John 2:4–6).

We who are in Christ live "for the Lord" (14:7–12), not to gratify everyone's personal expectations. This cannot mean that it does not matter what we believe, nor can it mean that we do not consider one another in what we do (recall 12:9–10; see Phil. 2:3–4). Rather, it means that our Master is Christ, and He measures our work, not someone else. Christ did not die and rise from the dead just so that we could judge each other; He did these things so that we might live to Him (14:9). If we attempt to "stand" on our own convictions (i.e., by using them as a test of Christian fellowship) rather than on Christ, then it will not go well for us when we "stand" in the judgment (14:10).

Seeking Peace, Not Creating Division (14:13–23): Instead of critiquing and condemning other Christians' personal convictions, the "strong" are to refrain from putting such stumbling blocks before the weak (14:13). An "obstacle" is any kind of unnecessary hindrance; a "stumbling block" is a trap or snare, something deliberately laid down in one's path to trip him up (i.e., to cause him to sin against his conscience).[76] Two Christians may have completely different convictions about what is proper to eat, for example, yet both can be justified by faith in God.

For example, Paul knows that eating meat (specifically, meat that is sacrificed to an idol; see 1 Cor. 10:24–33) is not unlawful, since "nothing is unclean in itself" (14:14). However, he would not exercise this Christian liberty of his *if* it caused another Christian to violate his conscience: he would refrain from eating meat in the company of one who (because of his lack of knowledge) believed it would be sinful to do so.[77] Not everything lawful is automatically edifying; not everything permissible is always wise or compassionate (1 Cor. 10:23–24). We are to be sensitive to the limited knowledge and tender consciences of those who are weak in faith. "Do not destroy with your food"—or with any other matter of personal opinion—"him for whom Christ died" (14:15; see 1 Cor. 8:9–13).

This entire section (14:1–23) certainly speaks of Christian liberties: where they exist and where (or when) they must be set aside. One's Christian liberty is a "good thing" but can be "spoken of as evil [lit., blasphemed]" if not exercised properly (14:16). The spiritual matters of God's kingdom must be more important than one's personal preferences, liberties, or opinions

(14:17). Being "acceptable" to God must be more important than being self-approved (14:18); being "approved by men"—i.e., having a good reputation among the brethren—must be more important than imposing one's private convictions upon another. Christians are to pursue what makes for peace and edification among fellow believers (14:19). God's "work" in a believer is far too important to "tear down" or jeopardize because of human convictions about far lesser things (14:20–21).

"The faith which you have…" (14:22)—this obviously cannot be *the* faith (the gospel); Paul is dealing here with private opinions and expendable liberties, not theology. Rather, he means: "What you do in faith, believing that it is to the glory of God, do it with full conviction and do not violate it." This does not mean one's beliefs cannot change, but that God recognizes that person's faith in Him for what it is and will accept it. One who knows what is wrong *for him* but partakes of it anyway violates his conscience and is self-condemned (14:23). Yet, one is "happy," "blessed," or approved by God, if what he does agrees with his conscience *and* God's law.

The "Strong" and "Weak" Are to Work Together (15:1–13): "Strong" (15:1) does not mean humanly superior, but learned, spiritually mature, "trained to discern good and evil" (Heb. 5:14), and having knowledge tempered with love (1 Cor. 8:1–3). The strong Christian has a moral responsibility to conduct himself appropriately toward a weak(er) Christian. But such respect and deference are to be mutual (as indicated by "Each of us"—15:2). Thus, it is the responsibility of the weak to listen to, learn from, and imitate those who are strong in the Lord (1 Cor. 11:1, Heb. 13:7). Every Christian begins as a weak Christian, but none of us should ever be content to remain one.

As always, "edification" is the goal (15:2): the building up of one another in love (1 Cor. 14:26b). Christ exemplified the attitude of "pleasing" one's fellow believer—not gratifying his every *request* but accommodating his immature *faith*. No one is strong apart from Christ, and all of us are weak in comparison to Him; therefore, the Lord sees us all as equals (15:3; citation is from Psalm 69:9). Having just cited from the OT, Paul then explains that such things were written and preserved so that "we might have hope" (15:4). The "hope" here refers to the fact that if we practice those things which are of heavenly origin, we will enjoy positive results.

The fact that we all are equal in God's sight, all share the same hope, and all read the same inspired Scripture, means that we can glorify God with "one voice [or mouth]" (15:6). We cannot do this, however, unless we are of the "same mind" (15:6; recall comments on 12:16). We can all have the "same mind" whether we are strong or weak: the power of Christ and His unifying gospel can accomplish this among all those who submit to Him.

We cannot be of "one accord" if fractured or divided, or if we refuse to "accept one another" (15:7). Again, Paul cites the humble yet sublime example of Christ: He was a servant both to Jews ("the circumcision") *and* Gentiles (in that His ministry gave them access to God; see John 12:20–32). He has united both groups into one body (the church), all to the glory of God (Eph. 2:11–18). He has "confirm[ed] the promises given to Israel" (15:8), which have never failed. His benevolent mercy has also become the source of tremendous praise among the Gentiles (15:9–11). (The OT quotes are, in order, from Psalm 18:49, Deut. 32:43, and Psalm 117:1.) The "root of Jesse" (15:12) refers to Christ's fulfillment of the promise given to David, Jesse's son, by which both Jews and Gentiles are blessed (quote is from Isa. 11:10).

"Now may the God of hope fill you with all joy …" (15:13)—hope is one of the supreme benefits of a righteous life with God. One who believes in God may "abound in hope" because of the "power of the Holy Spirit." The Spirit gives life and meaning to one's hope in a future life with God: one sanctified by God's Spirit has every reason to be experience joy and peace.

Questions

1.) Regarding 14:1–5, is it necessary that every Christian have the exact same beliefs to have fellowship with Christ? With one another?

   a. Where do we draw the line? In other words, when do one's personal convictions interfere with his fellowship with God and (thus) his brethren?

   b. In the case where this line has not been crossed, how are you supposed to "accept" a Christian whose personal convictions are different than your own?

2.) While Christians are allowed to have different personal convictions among themselves, are these convictions to be permanent and even unchallengeable?

3.) We are supposed to glorify God "with one voice" (15:6). Imagine a choir, for example, in which every singer chooses to sing his own song at his own tempo and according to his own pitch. The result will not be a beautiful song but a wretched, painful noise.

   a. How might this illustration apply on, say, a congregational level (without any literal reference to singing)?

   b. What does God require of Christians (collectively) to glorify Him with one voice? (There are several answers.)

4.) Why is the "one another" principle among Christians (15:7) so important? Can we have fellowship with God without it?

Lesson Nineteen:
A Proper Regard for Paul's Ministry
(15:14–33)

Paul's Ministry to the Gentiles (15:14–21): Paul spoke highly of the Roman Christians; his letter does not seem to deal with any specific problem among them (15:14–15). Regardless, God divinely commissioned him to speak with apostolic authority concerning God's doctrine. He thus spoke boldly and unapologetically, as we see in this section. Even though such information may only be a reminder to those who hear it, it is still important (2 Peter 3:1–2).

Paul took his work among the Gentiles seriously and did not want such effort to be in vain (Gal. 2:2, 4:11, etc.). In fact, he likens himself to a public servant ("minister")[78] and then to a priest offering up a living and holy sacrifice to God ("ministering"), the Gentiles being that offering (15:16). "[S]anctified by the Holy Spirit" indicates that God has given divine approval to this ministry. While he is proud of his own accomplishments, Paul defers all glory to God (15:17–18): His divine proofs ("signs and wonders") are what authenticates his ministry (2 Cor. 12:12).

As a result of Paul's extraordinary efforts, many Jews and Gentiles have heard and obeyed the gospel, from Jerusalem into Illyricum, a Roman province north of Macedonia (also known as Dalmatia) (15:19). He was often a trailblazer and a planter, establishing churches where others had not, rather than building on the work of others (15:20–21; see 1 Cor. 3:5–9). The church in Rome was an exception to this, but Paul realized the far-reaching benefits of having a church of God succeed in one of the major hubs of the ancient world. The citation in 15:21 (from Isa. 52:15) speaks paradoxically to the greatness of a crucified King.

The Gentiles' Indebtedness to the Jews (15:22–33): "For this reason …" (15:22)—i.e., Paul here explains why he has not yet visited the church in Rome. He has been extremely busy traveling; he has had a great deal of work to do; he has a mission to take care of (detailed shortly). His delay was not for lack of desire but lack of time; also, difficult circumstances have hindered him from seeing these brethren (recall 1:11–13; see 1 Thess. 2:18). Having done what he could do in "these regions" (i.e., where he had already preached the gospel and established churches), he anticipated moving on to further regions (15:23).

Paul's immediate concern, however, is the collection of benevolence money from (predominantly) Gentile churches for the saints in Jerusalem (15:25–27). Paul did not reveal why the Jewish Christians were in such need, but there are legitimate reasons:

- Famine had hit several parts of the Roman Empire—and especially Palestine—during the reign of Emperor Claudius (AD 41–54).
- Christians in Jerusalem faced persecution from non-believing Jews there, which could have hindered employment and other opportunities enjoyed by the Jewish community.
- Families divided over the gospel (as Jesus predicted in Mat. 10:34–36), leaving some family members without any financial support.
- The gospel attracts the poor and the ostracized, as it continues to do today; these people may look to the church for their only means of support.

Paul admits an ulterior motive for this collection as well. He hopes to draw the Gentile and Jewish churches together, forcing them to realize how indebted they are to one another (see 1 Cor. 9:11 [in principle], and 2 Cor. 8:12–15). In receiving this gift from the Gentiles, the Jews could not accuse Paul of abandoning them, or claim that the Gentiles had no concern for their Jewish brethren.[79] The Macedonians' generosity is detailed in 2 Cor. 8:1–5: out of their own poverty, they did what they could to send money to Jerusalem. "Achaia" alludes to the Corinthians, who procrastinated in their original pledge to help, but (apparently) did provide financial assistance, at Paul's urging.

Once this money was delivered to the elders in Jerusalem (Acts 21:15–17), it is Paul's intention to travel to Spain in yet another missionary journey, stopping briefly in Rome on the way.[80] (Spain at this time was under Roman jurisdiction, and encompassed the entire Iberian Peninsula, which includes modern-day Spain and Portugal.) He is aware, however, that he has many enemies in Jerusalem, and anticipates trouble (15:30–33). Indeed, the Spirit has promised him "bonds and afflictions" there (see Acts 20:22–24); thus, he requests prayers on his behalf (as in Eph. 6:18–20, Col. 4:2–4).

Paul may have had no idea of the full extent of what would happen to him in Jerusalem. He would be arrested on false charges and spend some two years in Roman custody awaiting a fair trial. Unable to get such a trial in Jerusalem or Caesarea, he would appeal to Caesar (Acts 25:10–12). Thus, he would indeed come to Rome, but as a prisoner in chains, not as the free man that he was at the time he wrote this epistle. This must have been a humiliating experience for Paul—not only to be treated as a criminal, but for his imprisonment to be the Roman Christians' first actual glimpse of him.[81]

Questions

1.) Paul spoke of "the obedience of the Gentiles by word and deed" (15:18), referring to the demonstration of the Gentiles' conversion to God.

   a. Can we measure obedience by words alone? (Consider Mat. 7:21–23 and Luke 6:46 in your answer.)

   b. If someone today claims to have faith in God, then should not we expect to see his obedience to God's commandments? Please explain.

2.) Paul performed "signs and wonders, in the power of the Spirit" wherever he preached among the Gentiles (15:19). What was the purpose for these? (Consider Heb. 2:1–4 in your answer.) Are we to preach with "signs and wonders" today?

   a. If so, why aren't we performing them?

   b. If not, does this mean that the "power of the Spirit" is no longer active among us?

3.) Please read 2 Cor. 8—9 in conjunction with 15:25–29. Paul's benevolence campaign for Jerusalem might appear as though he was simply preaching for money.

   a. What measures did Paul take to respond to this perception? (Consider 1 Cor. 9:8–18 and 2 Cor. 2:17, for example.)

   b. Due to the risk of misrepresentation, should Paul have done nothing for the Jerusalem Christians?

   c. Should we act in others' best interests only when there is no danger of anyone misconstruing our intentions? Please explain.

Lesson Twenty: Paul's Greetings and Final Admonitions (16:1–27)

Ancient letters often included the author's "commendation" or personal endorsement of the one who carried it (see 2 Cor. 3:1). In the present case, Paul commends a Christian lady named Phoebe for this purpose (16:1–2). Apparently, Phoebe was a woman of some prominence, possibly a well-to-do widow, and is referred to in the Greek text as a deaconess [lit., *diakonos*, often translated here as "servant"]. Cenchrea is an ancient port town in Achaia a few miles east of Corinth (Acts 18:18).

Paul's Salutations to Various Brethren (16:3–16): This section is the longest list of greetings in the NT. Prisca and Aquila (16:3–4) are undoubtedly the same Priscilla and Aquila from Acts 18:1–3 and 18:24–26. Paul's last known epistle also mentions this couple (2 Tim. 4:19). They had rescued Paul from a life-threatening situation to their own endangerment. This sparing of Paul's life made it possible for him to bring the gospel message to many Gentiles. Notice in 16:5a that "the church" (i.e., a local congregation of believers) met in this couple's home, which is how most early Christians assembled for worship—in private homes, not church buildings.

There is little or nothing known about the rest of these people, except that their names are of Latin or Greek origin. Likely, these people were either Gentiles or Hellenized (Greek-cultured) Jews; many may have been, like Paul, Roman citizens. It is obvious that Paul was well-traveled to have known so many people, and that he had friends all over the known world.

The custom of greeting with a kiss (16:16) was a customary practice in the ancient world and continues in some countries today. This form of greeting compares to a handshake in our own American or Western European culture. The emphasis seems not to be on the practice itself (i.e., this is not a command to literally kiss one another) but speaks of the *nature* of it: the "kiss" is to be a holy one, not one given in deceit (think of Judas' kiss of betrayal) or with impropriety (see 1 Tim. 2:8 for a parallel idea). In other words, whatever form of greeting we use ought to be with genuineness and holiness, not with hypocrisy or ungodly motives.

The phrase "churches of Christ" (16:16) appears nowhere else in the NT. In several cases, Christ's churches are identified by where they are: "the church of God which is at Corinth" (1 Cor. 1:2, 2 Cor. 1:1); "the church which is at Cenchrea" (Rom. 16:1); "the church of the Laodiceans" (Col. 4:16); etc. Such expressions are descriptive, not authoritative: they define groups of people with a common identity and in a common locale. The phrase "church of Christ" is not a proper name, or a formal, official, or denominational title for Christ's churches. Indeed, the spiritual body of Christ is not comprised of churches (congregations), but only of individual members. While the brotherhood may use "churches of Christ" today to identify congregations with a common belief system, there is no authority to use this name alone as a test of fellowship for those who use another biblically acceptable name.

Paul closes this epistle with a strong admonition to be vigilant for dissenters within their own group (16:17). His objective is to promote "the bond of peace in the unity of the Spirit" (Eph. 4:3; recall 14:19); those who undermine that unity are divisive (1 Cor. 1:10–13). "Hindrance" [Greek, *skandalon*] is translated elsewhere as "offense" or "stumbling block": divisive people create a satanic obstacle to Christian fellowship (see Phil. 3:18–19). For this reason, they are to be "marked" or identified; their agenda is a self-serving and deceptive one, regardless of what they profess (16:18).[82]

There are, in every congregation, "the unsuspecting [or, innocent]"—those who are still tender and naïve toward the stratagems and manipulations of false teachers (2 Peter 2:18–19). Thus, while he rejoices over their success, Paul warns the Roman Christians not to become complacent toward or oblivious to danger (16:19). God's people are to be wise in what is good, not well-acquainted with evil; they are to be aware of danger, but not participating in dangerous activities that threaten their souls (Mat. 10:16, 1 Cor. 14:20). "The God of peace will soon crush Satan under your feet" (16:20)—whether this is a prophetic disclosure (as in Gen. 3:15 or 2 Tim. 4:3–5) or simply one based upon biblical history, the statement is true. God's people will be victorious over Satan if they choose God over any other source of deliverance (James 4:7–8).

Finally, Paul includes greetings from those who are traveling with him (16:21–23; see Acts 20:1–5). These names are also either Greek or Latin in origin; these people may have had ties to Rome or were personally acquainted with some Roman Christians. "Timothy" is undoubtedly the same protégé of Paul's to whom *1 & 2 Timothy* were written; he may also be the one who was later imprisoned (Heb. 13:23). "Jason" may have been the same man mentioned in Acts 17:5–9, and "Sosipater" may be the Sopater of Acts 20:4, but we cannot substantiate these conclusions.

"Tertius" was the amanuensis (i.e., a copyist or secretary) who penned this epistle at Paul's dictation; Paul honors him by allowing his personal greeting. "Gaius" may be the one mentioned in 1 Cor. 1:14, not the man from Derbe (Acts 20:4); whether he is the Gaius from John's epistles is unknown to us for certain, but it seems unlikely, given the span of time between the two epistles, and because Gaius was a very common name in Paul's day. "Erastus" was the "city treasurer"—i.e., of the city of Corinth—which indicates how deeply the gospel had penetrated through various social strata in that place. "Quartus" [Latin, "the fourth"] is unknown to us. Many scholars do not even acknowledge 16:24, as it is not in any of the earliest manuscripts; its redundancy (from 16:20b) is also conspicuous. Nonetheless, the content of this verse is neither contradictory nor questionable.

Paul fittingly closes this profound letter with a doxology—a hymn of praise to God (16:25–27). God entrusted the gospel to Paul to preach to all men (both Jews and Gentiles), in fulfillment of the "mystery" first declared by the OT prophets. Faith in God required faith in His gospel: this faith must be in "obedience" (recall 1:5 and 15:18), not merely a verbal profession. In all, we are to praise God for all He has done to save us from ourselves, the world's corruption (2 Peter 1:4), and law's condemnation of us as lawbreakers.

Paul ends this beautiful doxology with this: "To the only wise God, through Jesus Christ, be the glory forever. Amen." The "wisdom of God" is infinitely greater than the wisdom of men (1 Cor. 1:18–29); Jesus Christ has demonstrated this through the wisdom He revealed in His teaching.

Questions

1.) What stands out in 16:1–13 is not so much the names of Christians themselves, but the personal and expressive way in which Paul regards these people:

   - "our sister ... [who] has been a helper of many, and of myself as well"
   - "my fellow workers in Christ Jesus"
   - "my beloved" (or "the beloved" or "my beloved in the Lord")—several uses
   - "[she] has worked hard for you"
   - "my kinsmen and my fellow prisoners who are outstanding among the apostles"—"kinsmen" is most certainly used in a spiritual context here
   - "our fellow worker in Christ"
   - "the approved in Christ"
   - "my kinsman"—see comment above on "kinsmen"
   - "who are in the Lord"
   - "workers in the Lord"
   - "... who has worked hard in the Lord"
   - "a choice man in the Lord"

   What should these descriptors tell us about what Christ wants us to be busy doing?

   What should this also tell us about how we are to regard men and women who work hard "in the Lord" (see 1 Cor. 16:15–16, 1 Thess. 5:12–13, and Heb. 13:18–19)?

2.) Since Paul spoke against those who cause divisions (16:17), what exactly is in danger of being divided? (There is more than one answer.)

3.) Compare Paul's warning in 16:19 with those in Mat. 10:16, 1 Cor. 14:20, and 1 Thess. 5:4–6. Are these warnings as relevant today as they were in the first century? Why should spiritual wisdom (ideally) lead to moral innocence?

Sources Used for *Romans Personal Workbook*

Barnes, Albert. *Barnes' Notes on the New Testament*, vol. 10. Database © 2014 by WORDsearch Corp. (orig. published by Blackie & Son, London, 1885).

Barrett, C. K. *The Epistle to the Romans.* New York: Harper & Row, 1957.

Bruce, F. F. "Romans, Epistle to the." *The Zondervan Pictorial Encyclopedia of the Bible*, vol. 5. Merrill C. Tenney, gen. ed. Grand Rapids: Zondervan Publishing, 1976.

Coffman, James Burton. *Commentary on Romans.* Austin, TX: Firm Foundation Publishing House, 1973.

Hendriksen, William. *New Testament Commentary: Exposition of Paul's Epistle to the Romans.* Grand Rapids: Baker Book House, 1981.

Lard, Moses. *Commentary on Romans.* Delight, AR: Gospel Light Publishing Co., no date (orig. published 1863).

Lenski, R. C. H. *The Interpretation of St. Paul's Epistle to the Romans: Commentary on the New Testament.* Peabody, MA: Hendrickson Publishers, 1998.

Lipscomb, David. *A Commentary on the New Testament Epistles: Romans.* J. W. Shepherd, ed. Nashville, TN: Gospel Advocate Co., 1983.

Luther, Martin. *Commentary on Romans.* Translated by J. Theodore Mueller. Grand Rapids: Zondervan Publishing House, 1954.

McGuiggan, Jim. *The Book of Romans.* Lubbock, TX: Montex Publishing Co., 1982.

Robertson, A. T. *Word Pictures in the New Testament*, vol. 4 (electronic edition). © 1932, renewal © 1960, by the Sunday School Board of the Southern Baptist Convention; database © 2007 by WORDsearch Corp.

Strong, James. *Strong's Talking Greek-Hebrew Dictionary* (electronic edition). Database © 2004 by WORDsearch Corp.

Vincent, Marvin R. *Vincent's Word Studies in the New Testament*, vol. 3 (electronic edition). Database © 2014 by WORDsearch Corp.

Whiteside, R. L. *Commentary on Romans.* Denton, TX: Inys Whiteside, 1945.

Wuest, Kenneth S. *Word Studies in the Greek New Testament,* vol. 1. Grand Rapids: Eerdmans Publishing Co., 1955; reprinted, 1992.

Scripture taken from the NEW AMERICAN STANDARD BIBLE ®, Copyright © 1960, 1962, 1963, 1968, 1971, 1972, 1973, 1975, 1977, 1995 by The Lockman Foundation. Used by permission.

Endnotes

1   David Lipscomb, *A Commentary on the New Testament Epistles: Romans*, J. W. Shepherd, ed. (Nashville, TN: Gospel Advocate Co., 1983), 16.

2   Of course, this visit did not happen in the way Paul intended. We know that he did go to Rome, but only upon his appeal to Caesar Nero (ca. AD 61–62) as a prisoner in chains. This shows that Paul did sometimes form his own plans apart from being directed by the Spirit, and which the Spirit did not always allow him to carry out (adapted from R. L. Whiteside, *Commentary on Romans* [Denton, TX: Inys Whiteside, 1945]), 14.

3   Lipscomb argues that the ancient Gentiles did not have specific knowledge of God's will regarding their salvation, citing Eph. 2:12 and 1 Cor. 1:21 (Romans, 34–35). While this is true, it is not Paul's point. These ancients did not turn away from a codified plan of salvation; they turned away from God Himself. If they had not done this, then they would have sought God through those who did know Him (such as Noah, Melchizedek, Job, Jethro, etc.).

4   R. C. H. Lenski, *The Interpretation of St. Paul's Epistle to the Romans: Commentary on the New Testament* (Pea body, MA: Hendrickson Publishers, 1998), 92.

5   James Coffman, *Commentary on Romans* (Austin TX: Firm Foundation Publishing, 1973), 39.

6   We should note here also that ingratitude (the refusal to give thanks) and irreverence (turning away from God) go together: if one exists, so does the other. (The opposite is also true: genuine gratitude toward God will always manifest itself in genuine reverence for Him and vice versa.)

7   On this point, we cannot ignore God's unmistakable judgment against Sodom and Gomorrah for this very thing (Gen. 19). In 2 Peter 2:7, such people are called "unprincipled"—i.e., those who have no respect for law or authority; in Jude 1:7, they are described as having "indulged in gross immorality." Despite its growing acceptance and alleged normalcy today, the entire Bible explicitly and consistently condemns homosexual behavior.

8   The "wrath of God"—His settled, righteous anger—is against all such unrighteousness, and "comes upon the sons of disobedience" (Eph. 5:6). While today it is popular (and convenient) either to minimize this wrath

or dismiss it altogether, the gospel is clear and consistent concerning God's burning anger toward those who purposely and defiantly abandon His divine nature.

9   C. K. Barrett, *The Epistle to the Romans* (New York: Harper & Row, 1957), 38.

10   "God did not cause their impurity, but He abandoned them to the natural consequences of the lusts already working in them" (Lipscomb, *Romans,* 39).

11   Concerning "the darkness"—what it is, how it is so seductive, and why it is so powerful—I strongly recommend my book, *This World Is Not Your Home* (Spiritbuilding Publishers, 2022); go to www.spiritbuilding.com/chad.

12   See also 1 Cor. 6:9–10, 1 Tim. 1:10, 2 Peter 3:7, and Jude 1:7.

13   The "you" in 2:4–5 is used editorially, not accusatory. Paul is not saying, "You Roman Christians are doing what I am describing," but rather, "Anyone is capable of what I am describing, and those who do so will receive a corresponding punishment."

14   The phrase, "without the Law" (2:12), does not imply the complete absence of any law but a law different than that which governed the Jews; see similar expressions in 1 Cor. 9:19–21. In most cases in Romans, the definite article ("the") is not in the original Greek text. Thus, the capitalization of "Law" is at the discretion of the translators, since in the Greek text all letters are capitalized. A more accurate rendering of "the Law" would be "law"; yet in some cases, the context does imply the Law of Moses, or simply, "the Law."

15   Jim McGuiggan, *The Book of Romans* (Lubbock, TX: Montex Publishing Co., 1982), 103.

16   "Covenant" and "law" are not the same things, even though they are very closely related. Covenant defines the terms by which two or more parties can function as they mutually work toward a stated goal. Law—for those under covenant—describes the expected behavior or appropriate responses of those who are bound by covenant.

17   "My gospel" does not mean Paul owned the gospel of Christ any more than he owned God when he said "my God" (recall 1:8). He only means here "the gospel that I preach," as in 1 Cor. 15:1–2.

18 In fact, God sought from the Jews a circumcision of their hearts, not mere physical circumcision; see Deut. 10:16, Jer. 4:4, Acts 7:51, etc.

19 This point does not invalidate or render unnecessary circumcision, if indeed that is what God commanded. The emphasis here is on priority, not exclusivity. First, God says, in essence, "Get your heart right and thus put your faith in Me," for the one whose genuine faith is in God will certainly honor whatever else God has called him to do.

20 McGuiggan, *The Book of Romans*, 117; my paraphrase.

21 These quotes are from (in the order used): Psalm 14:1–3, 53:1–3, 5:9, 140:3, 10:7, Prov. 1:16, 1:15–16, Isa. 59:7–8, and Psalm 36:1. While Paul quotes (sometimes loosely) from the Septuagint—the Greek translation of the Hebrew OT (*ca.* 200 BC)—his own renderings of these passages are as authoritative as the ones from which they came.

22 James Strong, *Strong's Talking Greek-Hebrew Dictionary* (electronic edition) (database © 2004 by WORDsearch Corp.), G5420.

23 "Righteousness" and "justification" are related but not equal. "Righteousness" refers to being godly in one's conduct; it is a state of being which God confers upon a person who imitates His holy behavior. "Justification" is a legal term, which refers to one's innocence before God, the price for his innocence having been sufficiently satisfied by another (Christ). Both terms necessarily imply forgiveness, for one can be neither righteous nor justified otherwise (adapted from Barrett, *The Epistle to the Romans*, 75–76).

24 "Fall short" is an ever-present, infinitive, continuous phrase: each person continues to sin against God's holiness even after having done it once. Having sinned against law, we thereafter continue to fall short of being justified by that law. Jesus Christ is the only exception to this; having kept the Law of Moses perfectly, He has therefore completed (fulfilled) the Law (Mat. 5:17).

25 For a full study on "grace," I strongly recommend my book, *The Gospel of Saving Grace* (Spiritbuilding Publishers, 2020); go to www.spiritbuilding.com/chad.

26 "Propitiation" [Greek, *hilasterion*] is translated "mercy seat" in Heb. 9:5. "Mercy seat" refers to the lid of the ark of the covenant; once a year it was sprinkled with blood on the Day of Atonement (Lev. 16). The fact that we are sprinkled with Jesus' blood (1 Pet. 1:2) leads us to conclude that

He has become to us the living substance of what the ancient mercy seat was to Israel: the union of earthly blood and divine mercy, which provides atonement for sins.

27 The traditional idea of God "rolling forward" His forgiveness of faithful people who lived prior to Christ's sacrifice is unbiblical. God did not "roll forward" His forgiveness; He forgave those people upon their having demonstrated faith in Him (through obedience to whatever He required of them). The numerous passages in Leviticus, for example, in which the Israelite was forgiven (4:20, 26, 31, 5:10, 13, etc.), and David's own words (Psalm 32:1, 51:1–2, etc.), do not indicate a postponed forgiveness but a full and complete one. In other words, God was so confident that His Son would be the perfect sacrifice for sin, He forgave people in full even before Christ's blood for that forgiveness had not yet been shed (on His cross).

28 Literally, "apart from law"—there is no definite article here in the Greek text (Whiteside, *Commentary*, 75).

29 "Tribulations" refers to "pressures," but means troubles, persecutions, or burdens (Strong, *Dictionary* [electronic], G2347); see John 16:33 and Acts 14:22.

30 Lenski, *Interpretation*, 338.

31 "Reconciliation" is from a Latin base (*reconcilio*), but the Greek word Paul uses here is *katallasso*, "to change mutually; to compound a difference" (Strong, *Dictionary* [electronic], G2644).

32 Moses Lard notes that we are reconciled to God, not the other way around: God does not change, but we are changed by Him. We once were disobedient and enemies; now we in Christ are obedient and friends of God (*Commentary on Romans* [Delight, AR: Gospel Light Publishing Co., no date; orig. published 1863], 159).

33 The "Doctrine of Original Sin," which has been incorporated into Calvinism, claims that all people are born guilty of Adam's sin—the "original sin"—and therefore are condemned by God upon birth. This assumes that we are all inherently corrupted and have a sinful nature (a.k.a. "total hereditary depravity") and is the purported basis for baptizing babies and young children.

34 The idea that we all have a "sinful nature," and that this is what causes us to sin, misrepresents the reality of our situation. Our "nature" is not

determined by Adam or sin but by our own personal choices to succumb, eventually, to our own lustful desires rather than to honor the moral code that God has built into our conscience (James 1:13–16; recall comments on 2:12–16). Some say, "We are sinners because we are the sons of a sinner. A sinner can beget only a sinner, who is like him" (Martin Luther, *Commentary on Romans* [Grand Rapids: Zondervan Publishing House, 1954], 95). But this confuses the father's guilt for his own sin and the effect of that guilt upon his posterity, versus the communication or transmission of such guilt. This also would require that Jesus was "a sinner," since He was born as a Man into humanity—a blasphemous idea. Even the Law of Moses says a man can be perfectly sinless—and justified by law—if he keeps the Law perfectly (Lev. 18:5; see Gal. 3:12). A perfectly law-abiding man cannot be born sinful and at the same time justified by law.

35 The physical curse remains for as long as we are bound to a physical system. Even though Christ has saved our souls, our bodies are still destined to die—the result of the curse upon Adam and his posterity. But we are promised that, once we are in God's world, we will never die but will have eternal life (John 11:25–26, 1 John 2:25).

36 Paul does not say that every person is automatically guilty of Adam's sin, any more than he says that every person is automatically saved by Christ's righteousness. He is drawing a contrast between the two men and their actions, not removing our personal responsibility or accountability to God for our actions.

37 "Baptism" [Greek, *baptizo*] means "to be whelmed (fully wet)"; immersion (in water) (Strong, *Dictionary* [electronic], G907). For a full study on "baptism," I recommend my book, *Being Born of God: The Role and Significance of Baptism in Becoming a Christian* (Spiritbuilding Publishers, 2014); go to www.spiritbuilding.com/chad.

38 In the same way, both circumcision and the Sabbath were signs of the covenant between God and Israel. Yet, God required these signs to be observed. Failure to keep the "sign of the covenant" indicated a disregard for the laws that commanded such observances, and the God who gave such laws (Gen. 17:14, Ezek. 20:19–21). This principle also applies to baptism: even though it serves as a sign of our covenant with God (Col. 2:9–12), it is also a command of God to those who wish to call upon His name (Acts 2:38, 10:48, and 22:16).

39 Many denominational commentators say of baptism, in so many words, "It is not essential, but it is important." This begs the question: why would God give us important instructions that are not essential? Who decided that this action is important but not essential? It was certainly not Paul.

40 For a much fuller study on this subject, I strongly recommend by book, *The New Testament Pattern: God's Plan for Christians and Their Churches* (Spiritbuilding Publishing, 2023); go to www.spiritbuilding.com/chad.

41 It is not necessary here for Paul to expound upon any exceptions to this, as in the case of immorality (Mat. 19:9) or abandonment (1 Cor. 7:15). His purpose is only to discuss the effect that physical death has on an earth-bound relationship. His case in point is marriage, but his primary explanation has to do with one's severance from sin (through having died to it) to become legally bound to Christ.

42 For an in-depth study of the Spirit and His work, I recommend my book, *The Holy Spirit of God: A Biblical Perspective* (Spiritbuilding Publishers, 2010); go to www.spiritbuilding.com/chad.

43 This "likeness" calls to mind the bronze serpent incident in Num. 21:6–9. The Israelites, because of their sinning against God, were bitten by serpents; God told Moses to put a likeness of the serpent—in reality, a likeness of the affliction—upon a pole, so that those bitten could look upon the bronze serpent and be healed. This is a "type" prophecy of what Christ did, which He Himself cited (John 3:14–15). The serpent(s) did not literally become bronzed any more than Jesus literally became a sinner; in both cases, a representative figure was used.

44 While Jesus died for us, God did not punish Him for us. The animals sacrificed to God under the Law of Moses were not being punished; they were slain as a representative of the one for whom they died. So it is with Christ: men punished Him for His alleged crimes, but God found Him completely innocent. An innocent man is not deserving of punishment, and God never punishes innocent people.

45 See also 2 Cor. 3:17 and 1 Peter 1:10–12, where the same interchangeable usage also occurs. In a parallel (but not exact) scenario, Paul describes Timothy as a "kindred spirit" who knows Paul's heart better than anyone else (Phil. 2:20–22). It might be said, then, that Paul's spirit and Timothy's spirit were united on one purpose and given over to the same

work, which seems to be what Paul is saying about the Holy Spirit being both "of God" and "of Christ" all at once.

46 Gender is irrelevant here. The reason for the "son" designation has to do with a right to an inheritance rather than a male or female distinction.

47 The unnaturalness of our sonship to God is evident in the fact that we are "born again" (John 3:3, 1 Peter 1:3). It is natural to be born once; to be "born again" is entirely unnatural and defies every expectation of life as we know it in the physical universe. Thus, we are made sons only through a supernatural process—one which transcends every natural process—and yet this adoption still guarantees that we will be heirs of God.

48 Lexicographers and commentators are nearly split on whether the word here should be "creation" or "creature." Lenski chooses to replace "creation" in this passage with "creature world" (*Interpretation*, 534).

49 The following points are cited in William Hendriksen's *The New Testament Commentary: Exposition of Paul's Epistle to the Romans* [Grand Rapids: Baker, 1981], 266; a similar list is found in Lard, *Commentary*, 269.

50 To our knowledge, angels either live in God's presence, or live in an irretrievably condemned state of being; there is no intermediate existence or expectation of salvation (Heb. 2:16).

51 Marvin R. Vincent, *Vincent's Word Studies in the New Testament*, vol. 3 (electronic edition) (database © 2014 by WORDsearch Corp.), on 8:20.

52 This does not mean—and does not have to mean—that God will restore the physical world to the paradise-like state in which it was originally made. Such is the teaching of Premillennialists and other literalists and semi-literalists who believe that God's intention is to restore the earth so that humans can live here forever, as in the beginning. But God has made it clear that the redeemed will live in God's world (John 14:1–3, Phil. 1:23, 1 Thess. 4:17, etc.). Furthermore, the physical creation will "pass away" (Mat. 24:35, 2 Peter 3:10–12, 1 John 2:15–17, etc.), as it is corrupted with sin and must be destroyed. Jesus did not die to save the physical creation but human souls. The souls of the redeemed will be the only remnant of this physical life that will enter heavenly glory.

53 Lenski, *Interpretation*, 536.

54 "[Christians'] redemption in Christ will not be completed until their bodies are raised from the dead and glorified and are become like Jesus in

His glorified and immortal state" (Lipscomb, *Romans*, 155). While Paul does not mention bodily resurrection here, this does seem to be the underlying thought.

55 "It is uncertain whether Paul means unspoken or unspeakable groans" (Barrett, *The Epistle to the Romans*, 168; emphasis his). Admittedly, we are denied a fuller explanation on this than what is provided here.

56 A. T. Robertson, *Word Pictures in the New Testament,* vol. 4 (electronic edition) (© 1960 by the Sunday School Board of the Southern Baptist Convention; database © 2007 by WORDsearch Corp.), on 8:26; Kenneth Wuest, *Word Studies in the Greek New Testament,* vol. 1 (Grand Rapids: Eerdmans Publishing Co., 1955), 140.

57 Being "called" necessarily implies that an invitation has been offered and (in this case) a response was made. God calls us through His gospel (1 Cor. 1:9, 2 Thess. 2:13–14, and 1 Peter 2:9); we call upon God through our response to it (compare Acts 2:21 and 2:39). This response must be accompanied by proper demonstrations of obedience (Acts 22:16, Rom. 10:9–13, etc.). "[T]hose who love the Lord" necessarily implies decisions made not by God but by all those who have believed in Christ.

58 In this passage, Paul states four great truths concerning Christ: He died (purposely and sacrificially); He was raised from the dead; He is now at the right hand of God; and He now intercedes for us. These four facts form the concrete basis for the Christian faith; without them, we have no gospel and no hope for the future.

59 "Not just: we shall conquer in the end; no, even now we are super-conquerors. And this not—let it be added immediately—by reason of our marvelous character and unflinching courage" (Hendriksen, *NTC*, 292).

60 The proportion may be likened to the small number of Jews who returned to Judea from Babylonian exile by the decree of Cyrus (2 Chron. 36:20–23). Consider the gospel a kind of heavenly "decree" of far greater value and significance, yet most Jews snubbed God's invitation into His kingdom. In His parables, Jesus expresses His own disappointment in His people (Mat. 21:33–43, 22:1–8, and Luke 14:16–24).

61 "To 'love' and 'hate' as God uses the terms means to approve or disapprove, to bless or curse" (Lipscomb, *Romans*, 172).

62 Paul quotes loosely from Deut. 30:11–14, where Moses reminded Israel that God's will was made evident to them through the Law that He had

revealed at Mt. Sinai (Deut. 29:29). Israel did not have to go searching for God's instructions; they only had to obey (in faith) what He said. Thus, even in the time of Moses, God's plan of justification by faith was already in full effect. While the Law of Moses could indeed justify a person who kept it perfectly (Lev. 18:5), no Israelite—save Christ Himself—did this. Furthermore, wherever there is justification by faith, there must be divine grace.

63 In fact, it is possible to believe without confessing (John 12:42–43), just as it is possible to confess without believing (Luke 6:46). In such cases, justification by faith is impossible because genuine faith has not yet been demonstrated.

64 The quote here is from Joel 2:32, the same as was cited by Peter in Acts 2:21 with reference to the "pouring out" of the Holy Spirit upon Christ's church. "Whoever" and "no distinction" (in 10:11–13) indicate that salvation has been extended to all people, regardless of ethnicity, genealogy, or gender.

65 Some commentators believe the "fullness of the Gentiles" refers to a particular number of Gentiles to be saved throughout history; once that quota is reached, humanity will be radically changed (or ended); see Hendriksen, *NTC*, 378; Lenski, *Interpretation*, 720; and Wuest, *Word Studies*, 199. Such interpretations seem unsupported and unnatural. Nowhere else in Scripture is there a reference to a set number of people to be saved.

66 Wuest, *Word Studies,* 206.

67 Lard, *Commentary,* 381.

68 In the Greek text, the entire passage of 12:6–18 is a series of imperative statements; Lenski believes each statement should be followed with an exclamation point (*Interpretation*, 758–77), and this makes sense. Thus, he renders these verses literally: "The love—not hypocritical! ... Rejoice in company with rejoicing ones! Weep with weeping ones!"—and so for the rest of Paul's brief admonitions in this chapter.

69 Strong, *Dictionary* (electronic), G5381.

70 Robertson, *Word Pictures* (electronic), on 12:21.

71 Lard, *Commentary,* 398.

72 Political revolution, such as what the American colonies pursued against Great Britain in 1776, is a special case. Paul's comments here address a general position, not special cases.

73 Whiteside, *Commentary*, 263.

74 Strong, *Dictionary* (electronic), G2970.

75 *Ibid.*, G2845. The Greek word here is *koite*, which means "bed" or "chambering"; it is the word from which we get "coitus," which means sexual intercourse.

76 "Obstacle" (14:13) is from *proskomma*, an offense or stone of stumbling. "Stumbling block" is from *skandalon*, from which we also get "scandalous." That which is offensive to a brother in Christ is scandalous to God: He finds such action shameful and unbecoming of His children. A stumbling block is not an accident but is a deliberate imposition or an intentional carelessness or unconcern for another's welfare.

77 The key to this passage involves determining what constitutes sin or not. It is not sinful to have a certain personal conviction about what you eat, or what religious day of the year you may honor, if these convictions do not conflict with what God has already determined in His gospel. There are two ways to sin against God: direct violation of His word and a violation of one's own conscience. This does not mean that conscience is equal to (or, on par with) God's word but that the two things provide a God-given moral compass by which a person may navigate through life. God's word never changes and cannot be altered; one's conscience, however, can change and can be recalibrated with a better understanding of God's word over time.

78 "The word here translated minister is not *diakonos*, the usual word for minister, or servant, but *leitourgos*, a word that usually had an official significance, one who performs a public service" (Whiteside, *Commentary*, 285).

79 This negative sentiment is expressed in James' comments to Paul in Acts 21:17–21, which chronologically follows very shortly after Paul penned these very words in Romans. Yet Barnes' comments are instrumental here: "Nothing tends so much to wear off prejudice, and to prevent unkind feelings in regard to others, as to set about some purpose to do them good, or to unite with them in doing good" (*Barnes' Notes on the New Testament*, vol. 10 [electronic edition; database © 2014 by WORDsearch Corp.], on 15:26; emphases are his).

80 In Paul's perspective, "Rome was not a goal but a place which he must visit in transit, or at best a base from which he could set out on a further phase of his ministry, with a view to repeating in the western Mediterranean

the program which (at the time indicated in Acts 19:21) he had almost completed in the East" (F. F. Bruce, "Romans," *The Zondervan Pictorial Encyclopedia of the Bible,* vol. 5 [Grand Rapids: Zondervan Publishing, 1976], 150).

81 "The reception of the letter [i.e., to the Romans] may have had something to do with the welcome he received from some Roman Christians as he approached their city along the Appian Way, when he was still some forty miles distant. 'The brethren there,' says his companion Luke, 'when they heard of us, came as far as the Forum of Appius and Three Taverns to meet us. On seeing them Paul thanked God and took courage' (Acts 28:15)" (Bruce, "Romans," 152; bracketed words are mine).

82 "This turning away amounted to a withdrawal of fellowship; and the withdrawal was to continue, so long as those withdrawn from continued to produce divisions. It was a separation of true brethren from false; and, without a reformation, it was final" (Lard, *Commentary,* 463).

www.ingramcontent.com/pod-product-compliance
Lightning Source LLC
Chambersburg PA
CBHW040322050426

42453CB00017B/2432